Cancún
Cozumel
Yucatán Peninsula

Fodor's 91

Cancún, Cozumel, Yucatán Peninsula

FODOR'S TRAVEL PUBLICATIONS, INC.
New York & London

Fodor's Cancún, Cozumel, Yucatán Peninsula

Editor: Kathleen McHugh
Contributors: Jim Budd, Maribeth Mellin, Jane Onstott, Wendy Ortiz de Montellano, Carolyn Price
Illustrations: Michelle LaPort
Maps: Dino Dinoir, Mark Stein Studios, Pictograph
Cover Photograph: Richard Pasley/Stock Boston

Cover Design: Vignelli Associates

Special Sales

Fodor's Travel Publications are available at special discounts for bulk purchases (100 copies or more) for sales promotions or premiums. Special editions, including personalized covers, excerpts of existing guides, and corporate imprints, can be created in large quantities for special needs. For more information, write to Special Marketing, Fodor's Travel Publications, 201 East 50th Street, New York, NY 10022. Inquiries from the United Kingdom should be sent to Fodor's Travel Publications, 20 Vauxhall Bridge Rd., London, England SW1V 2SA.

MANUFACTURED IN THE UNITED STATES OF AMERICA
10 9 8 7 6 5 4 3 2 1

CONTENTS

FOREWORD

For sun worshipers heading south of the border, first came Acapulco. Then followed Puerto Vallarta, Mazatlán, and other Pacific Coast resorts. Now it's time for Cancún and the Caribbean Coast of Mexico to share the limelight—or sunlight—in offering hedonistic pleasures.

Cancún is a product of the jet age but not solely for the jet set. Its fine beaches, hotels, and restaurants are there for all to enjoy. Nearby, the island of Cozumel, with an easy-going, relaxed atmosphere, beckons aquarians of every sign of the zodiac—its crystal-clear waters, abounding in marine life, delight divers and anglers alike. Meanwhile, Mérida, the capital of the Yucatán, offers all the charms of a colonial city.

Throughout the Yucatán Peninsula, antiquity coexists with modern life. Centuries-old Mayan ruins have been intriguing archaeologists for years, and in some areas of the Yucatán, the Maya culture and influence still continue to thrive.

Fodor's Cancún, Cozumel, Yucatán Penninsula is designed to help you plan your own trip based on your time, your budget, your energy, and your idea of what the trip should be. Perhaps after having read this guide you'll have some new ideas of your own. We have, therefore, tried to put together the widest possible *range* of activities and within that range to offer you *selections* that will be worthwhile, safe, and of good value. The descriptions we provide are designed to help you make your own intelligent choices from our selections.

While every care has been taken to assure the accuracy of the information in this guide, the passage of time will always bring change, and consequently the publisher cannot accept responsibility for errors that may occur.

All prices and opening times quoted here are based on information available to us at press time. Hours and admission fees may change, however, and the prudent traveler will avoid inconvenience by calling ahead.

Fodor's wants to hear about your travel experiences, both pleasant and unpleasant. When a hotel or restaurant fails to live up to its billing, let us know and we will investigate the complaint and revise our entries where the facts warrant it.

Send your letters to the editors of Fodor's Travel Publications, 201 E. 50th Street, New York, NY 10022.

FACTS AT YOUR FINGERTIPS

FACTS AT YOUR FINGERTIPS

FACTS AND FIGURES. Flat as a tortilla, unscarred by rivers, Mexico's 55,000-square-mile Yucatán Peninsula juts out like a thumb from the rest of the country, washed on its west and north by the Gulf of Mexico and on its east by the Caribbean Sea. To the south it borders on Belize (formerly British Honduras). Three states comprise the area: Yucatán proper, Quintana Roo (both covered in this volume), and Campeche.

In many ways the peninsula is a different country. Where most of Mexico is rugged mountains, vast deserts, and splendid forests, Yucatán is a limestone cap covered with scrub. Where most of Mexico considers itself Aztec, Yucatán is Mayan. For most of its history the peninsula was isolated from the rest of the republic and went its own, more or less separate, way.

Mérida, capital of Yucatán state, with 700,000 inhabitants, is by far the largest city in the peninsula, although the new resort city of Cancún, home to nearly 200,000 people, may surpass it by the turn of the century. Chetumal, where about 100,000 live down near the Belize border, is capital of Quintana Roo (pronounced KIN-ta-na Row). Cozumel, a few miles off the peninsula's eastern shore, is Mexico's largest island and one of the country's favorite resorts.

CLIMATE. Hot is what Yucatán usually is. There are exceptions, of course. Occasional cold snaps blow up during the winter and once in a while the coastal areas can get quite breezy. April and May can be exceptionally steamy. In the summer, afternoon rains generally cool things a bit and autumn along the Quintana Roo coast can be stormy at times.

POPULATION. The Mayas of old, descendants of the builders of Uxmal and Tulum, live on in Yucatán and give the area its special flavor. Physically they appear to be a race apart, short and squat of stature and famed throughout the rest of Mexico for their rather prominent heads. They are also noted as being exceptionally friendly and hospitable.

It might be said that the Mayas never were conquered. The Spaniards, after considerable difficulty, managed to establish themselves around Mérida and lay out vast plantations, but great numbers of Mayas simply retreated into the scrub and lived on in little villages as their forefathers had done for centuries before Columbus was born. To this day, many continue to live in the traditional oval huts, sleep in hammocks, and speak the ancient tongue.

The Spaniards and their descendants who settled around Mérida ruled as a feudal aristocracy until perhaps half a century ago. Their palatial mansions along the city's Paseo Montejo stand now as fading monuments to a vanished age.

In recent years some outsiders from the mainland as well as immigrants from the Middle East have moved in, but overall the Yucatán Peninsula remains the land of the Mayas.

LANGUAGE. Spanish is the official language, although Maya is heard more frequently in the villages. English is understood at most Mérida and

1

resort-area hotels, but not always. Efforts by visitors to speak Spanish are always appreciated.

WHERE TO GO. The beaches and the archaeological zones are what bring travelers to the Yucatán Peninsula.

The Mexican Caribbean along the coast of Quintana Roo is the biggest attraction. Cancún, which had nary a hotel until 1974, is, for many people, first choice when it comes to a Mexican holiday. Cozumel, a 30-mile-long island just over the horizon with wonderful diving in tequila-clear waters, is less glitzy than Cancún and, consequently, less expensive. More casual still are Isla Mujeres, an hour by boat from Cancún, and the tiny resorts that dot the shore between Cancún and Tulum.

Tulum, virtually inaccessible as recently as 1970, today is the most visited archaeological site in Mexico. It is just 80 miles from Cancún, and it features the ruins of a fortified seaside city that was still inhabited when the first Spanish explorers reached this part of the world. More dedicated Maya buffs may want to drive on inland from Tulum to Cobá, a classic Mayan city on the shores of five small lakes. Chichén Itzá, one of the most spectacular of the ancient centers, can be visited in a day trip from Cancún. Uxmal, Sayil, Labna, and other ruins are better seen on excursions out of Mérida.

Mérida is more than just a place to spend the night between archaeological tours. The city is one of the most attractive and romantic in all of Mexico, marvelous for strolling and stepping out at night. There is also a popular beach at Progreso, 21 miles north of Mérida.

Chetumal, on the southeastern corner of the peninsula, has a special appeal for those who seek out unusual places. Founded in 1898, it is one of the newest cities in the country and capital of one of the newest states. Duty-free shopping (Chetumal is the gateway to Belize) is a principal activity. There are beaches, lagoons, and Maya ruins nearby as well as an old Spanish fortress.

PLANNING YOUR TRIP. Even for experienced travelers, group tours and prepaid packages might be well worth looking into. Going in a group, especially on a chartered aircraft, means you will be paying only a fraction more than wholesale prices while perhaps sacrificing some independence. With a prepaid package, there is more freedom, yet costs are lower than when transportation, accommodations, and excursions are purchased separately.

In addition to lower costs, group tours and prepaid packages have another major plus: travelers have a helping hand available, should they need it once they arrive. Independent tourists have almost nowhere to turn in case of accident, theft, or illness.

When considering a package or group tour, you must be sure to study the fine print carefully. Those going abroad for the first time will appreciate the hand-holding group travel provides, but missing a plane, especially if it is a charter, may mean losing the price of the ticket. Packages may include more than you want or less than you want: free scuba will do no good if you are not a certified diver; if you really want to explore Uxmal and Chichén Itzá, opt for a package that overnights at the site rather than one where you go out and back in a day.

Among the items to check when considering any group tour or prepaid package are these:

• Is airfare included or are these only land arrangements? (Often when the price is for land arrangements, the operator may be able to offer attractive air fares.)

• Are taxes and tips part of the deal? If not, how much will they add to your costs?

• Are all meals, some meals, or no meals included?

• If a rental car is part of the package, will it be air-conditioned with automatic transmission, or will it be a standard-shift subcompact cooled by opening the windows? Are taxes, fuel, and insurance included?

• Does the operator specify in which hotel you will be lodged, or hedge by mentioning only "luxurious" or "superior" accommodations?

• What is the tour operator's responsibility for getting you home on time? Charter flights have been known to be canceled. When that happens, who picks up the tab if you must stay over an extra night or if you must obtain space on a scheduled carrier?

Tours and packages are sold through travel agents. It is important to find a reputable agent; membership in ASTA, the American Society of Travel Agents, is one good recommendation. Travel agents depend largely on repeat business and word-of-mouth advertising so they try to keep their clients happy.

Planning, of course, also involves deciding when to go and what to carry. What to carry is less of a problem when traveling to warm, sunny Yucatán where informality is the rule. When to go may depend on when one can go, but travelers should keep in mind that both weather (autumn can be stormy along the Caribbean) and prices (winter is expensive) vary according to season. When demand is heavy, say during Christmas week and in February, overbooking at the beach resorts can be a problem.

TAKING MONEY TO MEXICO. Credit cards, especially those issued by banks, are accepted as widely in Mexico as in the United States. Even so, a wad of $20 traveler's checks is nice to have stashed away. These should be cashed sparingly since the exchange rate does fluctuate (although the peso has been fairly stable for over a year). Also, it's just not safe to carry large sums of cash. While the Yucatán Peninsula is almost free of crime, using hotel safe deposit boxes is always a good idea.

Banks and exchange houses *(casas de cambio)* offer the best rates for dollars. Both U.S. and Canadian currency and traveler's checks are prized in Mexico; getting pesos for other monies tends to be a bit more complicated. At press time (April 1990), the peso was devaluating at the rate of 1 peso per day and the exchange rate was around 2,780 to the dollar.

INSURANCE. All kinds of policies are available, ranging from those covering air travel (often included automatically when a ticket is paid for by a credit card) to health, accident, and lost baggage (the latter may be difficult to obtain and more difficult to collect; best bet is to lock luggage, make certain there is ID both inside and outside, and carry everything of great value with you, including documents and jewelry).

It is wise to check your own health and accident policies to see whether you are covered abroad and how you can collect if any expenses are incurred. If you do need insurance, some organizations you may wish to check are:

Carefree Travel Insurance, Box 310, 120 Mineola Blvd., Mineola, NY 11501 (800–343–3533). Policies, available from many travel agents, include emergency medical evacuation.

International SOS Assistance, Inc., Box 11568, Philadelphia, PA 19116 (800–523–8930). Fees run from $25 for 7 days to $195 for a year.

International Association for Medical Assistance to Travelers (IAMAT), 417 Center St., Lewiston, NY 14092 (716–754–4883), and 40 Regal Rd., Guelph, Ont. N1K 1B5, Canada (519–836–0102). There is no fee for this service.

Trip cancellation insurance, available from travel agents, is an excellent idea when cancellation would otherwise result in loss of deposits, cost of air tickets, etc.

Motorists in Mexico always should carry third-person coverage; without it an accident may be followed by a stay in jail while responsibility is determined. U.S. insurance is not valid in Mexico, but Mexican insurance may be obtained at the border. It is also available in the U.S. from *Sanborn's Mexico Insurance Service,* Box 1210, McAllen, TX 78502 (512–686–0711). Insurance for rental cars is also available.

HOW TO GET THERE. By Air. Cancún, Cozumel, and Mérida all have international airports with service from several U.S. gateways. Frequently promotional fares are available and often package prices are lower than the cost of an ordinary ticket. With rates changing so frequently and so many specials (2 for the price of 1½, midweek discounts, etc.), consulting a travel agent is wise when saving money is important.

Travelers with flexible schedules sometimes can benefit from last-minute efforts tour and charter operators make to fill their planes. There are a number of brokers who specialize in discount sales; they charge an annual membership fee, usually under $50. Among these are *Moment's Notice,* 40 E. 49th St., New York, NY 10017 (212–486–0503); *Discount Travel International,* 114 Forrest Ave., Narberth, PA 19072 (215–668–2182); and *Worldwide Discount Travel Club,* 1674 Meridian Ave., Miami Beach, FL 33139 (305–534–2082). At times charter and tour operators advertise last-minute specials in Sunday newspaper travel supplements; some of these are more reliable than others.

Vacationers who prize comfort and are willing to pay for it may prefer to fly business class or first class, although these are not available on all flights into Yucatán airports.

By Bus. Backpackers and the like arrive in the Yucatán Peninsula by bus daily, some from Texas, others from Guatemala by way of Belize. Big appeals are the remarkably low fares and the opportunity to really see the country. Negatives include the language barrier, rather minimal comfort, and the need to purchase tickets shortly before departure at many depots, hoping that space will be available (no standees are carried on first-class buses; second-class buses are locals that stop everywhere).

By Ship. Cozumel is a major port of call for many Caribbean cruise vessels, some of these stopping at Playa de Carmen on the peninsula mainland. Few passengers, however, use these ships for one-way travel.

TIPS TO THE MOTORIST. With unleaded fuel scarce in Mexico, few American motorists are willing to risk their automobile engines on a 2,500-mile, round-trip journey into the Yucatán. The roads, after all, are only passing fair, spare parts may be hard to come by, and Mexican insurance can run $150 a month (U.S. policies are not valid south of the border).

Those who are contemplating a motor trip might also keep the following points in mind:

- Insurance should be considered mandatory; uninsured motorists involved in accidents may be held in jail until responsibility is determined and, if found at fault, released only after damages are paid.
- If you enter Mexico with a car, you must leave with a car; possession of a vehicle is noted on one's tourist card. If an emergency arises and you need to fly out, the auto must be left in the care of Mexican customs, a complicated and sometimes costly procedure.
- Distances and speed limits are given in kilometers; 110 k/h (68 mph) is the usual maximum speed on toll highways while 40 k/h (25 mph) is usual in towns where speed bumps lie waiting to bounce the unwary. All roads leading to and around the peninsula are two-lane blacktop in varying states of repair.
- Many towns have one-way streets, an arrow on the side of street-corner buildings indicating the way traffic flows. Two-headed arrows indicate two-way streets.
- A circle bearing an E with a slash through it (Ɇ) means no parking. License plates may be removed from illegally parked vehicles; they will be returned on payment of a fine.
- Road signs are similar to those in the United States but the wording is in Spanish: *alto* means stop; *no rebase,* no passing; *ceda el paso,* yield; *conserva su derecha,* keep right; *despacio,* slow; *tramo en reparación,* road work ahead; *desviación,* detour; and *no hay paso,* road closed.
- Major highways are patrolled by the Green Angels, bilingual mechanics driving green trucks who can replace broken fan belts, replenish empty fuel tanks, or at least provide a push into town. A service of the Tourism Ministry, the Green Angels charge only for parts and gasoline that may be needed, although tips are appreciated.
- Avoid driving at night. Free-grazing cattle are enough of a menace during the day. Some detours are dangerous after dark and with no Green Angels on the road until sunup, a breakdown means being stranded for hours.
- The only gasoline sold everywhere in Mexico is Pemex Nova, which contains lead. Pemex stations tend to be few and far between so never let the tank level get very low. Neither credit cards nor dollars are accepted at most service stations. *Lleno* "YEH-no" means fill it up and *aceite* "ah-SAY-tay" will get the oil checked (several U.S. brands of motor oil are available as well as Pemex's *Faja de Oro*). If you want the tire pressure checked, indicate *las llantas* "lahs YAN-tas"; the windshield is *parabrisas* "PAR-ah-BREE-sas" and will be cleaned only upon request. Service station attendants expect a tip; the equivalent of a dime will be fine. Rest rooms are usually filthy.
- Major repairs can be a problem, especially for auto models not sold in Mexico and for which there are no spare parts. In choosing a mechanic, your best course is to seek advice from your hotel whenever possible.
- Leave aiding accident victims to others. This goes against one's instincts, but under the Mexican legal system providing assistance can lead to unpleasant complications.

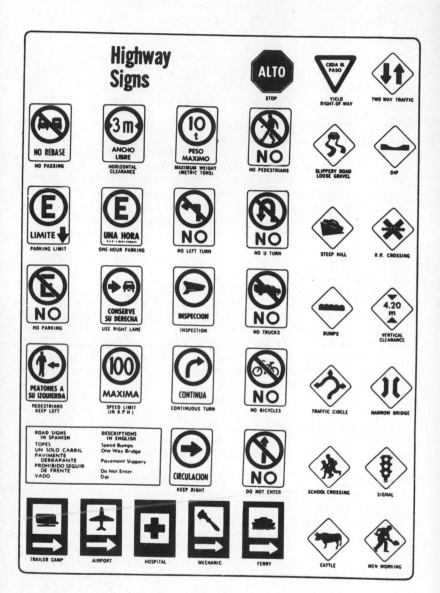

Highway Signs

STOP

YIELD RIGHT-OF-WAY

TWO WAY TRAFFIC

NO REBASE — NO PASSING

3 m ANCHO LIBRE — HORIZONTAL CLEARANCE

10 t PESO MAXIMO — MAXIMUM WEIGHT (METRIC TONS)

NO — NO PEDESTRIANS

SLIPPERY ROAD LOOSE GRAVEL

DIP

E LIMITE — PARKING LIMIT

E UNA HORA — ONE-HOUR PARKING

NO — NO LEFT TURN

NO — NO U TURN

STEEP HILL

R.R. CROSSING

E NO — NO PARKING

CONSERVE SU DERECHA — USE RIGHT LANE

INSPECCION — INSPECTION

NO — NO TRUCKS

BUMPS

4.20 m — VERTICAL CLEARANCE

PEATONES A SU IZQUIERDA — PEDESTRIANS KEEP LEFT

100 MAXIMA — SPEED LIMIT (IN K.P.H)

CONTINUA — CONTINUOUS TURN

NO — NO BICYCLES

TRAFFIC CIRCLE

NARROW BRIDGE

ROAD SIGNS IN SPANISH	DESCRIPTIONS IN ENGLISH
TOPES	Speed Bumps
UN SOLO CARRIL	One Way Bridge
PAVIMENTE DERRAPANTE	Pavement Slippery
PROHIBIDO SEGUIR DE FRENTE	Do Not Enter
VADO	Dip

CIRCULACION — KEEP RIGHT

NO — DO NOT ENTER

SCHOOL CROSSING

SIGNAL

TRAILER CAMP

AIRPORT

HOSPITAL

MECHANIC

FERRY

CATTLE

MEN WORKING

Rental cars are available for those who lack either the inclination or the time to drive down from the border. *Avis, Budget, Hertz,* and *National* as well as many local firms have cars for hire. Most readily available are Volkswagen and Nissan standard-shift models, although Ford, Chrysler, Chevrolet, and Jeep vehicles are manufactured in the country. Air-conditioned cars (a blessing in the steamy Yucatán) with automatic transmission should be reserved in advance. Rates are considerably higher for rental cars in Mexico than in the U.S. To help your driving in Mexico, we've included a page of highway signs and what they mean.

TRAVEL DOCUMENTS. U.S. citizens are required to have a tourist card—available from Mexican consulates, travel agents, or airlines serving the country—as well as proof of citizenship such as a birth certificate, voter registration card, or passport. The same regulations apply to Canadians.

British subjects need a valid passport and a Mexican tourist card. Passport may be secured from the Passport Offices in London; from passport offices in Glasgow, Liverpool, Newport, and Peterborough; or from any consulate abroad. It is valid for ten years. A Mexican tourist card may be secured from the Mexican Embassy, 8 Halkin St., London SW1; or, if already abroad, from any Mexican embassy and national airlines. Students wishing to study in Mexico and business travelers must inquire at the consulate for additional requirements. A passport or other proof of citizenship must be presented to reenter Great Britain. There is no limit on the amount of money carried out of the country for pleasure travel.

TRAVEL AGENTS. One should select a travel agent with the same care one chooses a physician, attorney, or stock broker. A vacation trip is, after all, a large investment and the cost, one hopes, will exceed those for one's medical and legal expenditures during a year.

In North America, the services of a travel agent are free save for out-of-pocket expenses. Their earnings are based on commissions paid by tour operators, airlines, hotels, and car-rental firms. While this leads some to tout costly holidays and organizations that pay the highest commissions, good agents seek to provide value and satisfaction for their clients, counting in return on repeat business and word-of-mouth recommendations.

European travel agents simply charge their clients a small fee and thus may be less biased in their recommendations.

In addition to honesty, good travel agents should be familiar with the area they are selling. They should, for example, be able to tell a pair of female clients where they can find an active social life or advise honeymooners where the most romantic spots are. Likewise, they should know enough not to pack a weary businessman off to a hotel where noise from the disco will seep into his room.

Group tours and prepaid packages usually are purchased through travel agents. Many kinds are available, and it takes an expert to know which particular program will best suit an individual client.

Membership in the American Society of Travel Agents (ASTA) is a good indication that a travel agent is a professional who knows his business. Many states require agents to be licensed, which is additional protection for the consumer. In Canada, Britain, and other countries, good travel agents belong to associations that police the ethics of their members.

TOUR OPERATORS. A number of organizations, known in the trade as wholesalers, offer a variety of package programs to Yucatán destinations. (Many hotel chains and airlines also have their own programs.) As mentioned previously, group tours usually offer the lowest prices, but even individual packages generally are much less expensive than an itinerary in which transportation, accommodations, and sightseeing excursions are purchased individually. Most tour operators market their packages only through retail travel agents, but since not all retailers handle all tour operators, you might wish to contact the various wholesalers to see what they have available.

Adventure Tours, 9818–B Liberty Rd., Randallstown, MD 21133 (301–922–7000).

American Express, Box 5014, Atlanta, GA 30302 (800–241–1700).

Asti Tours, 21 E. 40th St., New York, NY 10016 (800–223–7728).

Alexander Tours, 2607 Nostrand Ave., Brooklyn, NY 11210 (800–522–0457).

Apple Vacations, 25 N. West Point Blvd., Elkgrove, IL 60007 (800–365–2775).

Barbachano Tours, 1570 Madruga Ave., Penthouse, Coral Gables, FL 33146 (800–327–2254).

Betanzos OK Tours, 323 Geary St., Suite 418, San Francisco, CA 94102 (415–421–0955).

Cancún Hot-Line, Prestige Resort Hotel, Box 767, Lake Worth, FL 33460 (800–445–9008).

Cartan Travel, 2809 Butterfield Rd., Oak Brook, IL 60521 (800–422–7826).

Club Med, 3 E. 54th St., New York, NY (800–CLUB–MED).

Continental World Tours, 12101 S. Dixie Hwy., Miami, FL 33156 (800–327–3012).

First Family of Travel, 3530 Forest Lane, Dallas, TX 75234 (800–527–6366).

Firstours, 100 N. Sepulveda Blvd., El Segundo, CA 90245 (800–423–3118).

Flyfaire, 6 Skyline Dr., Hawthorne, NY 10532 (800–367–1036).

Four Winds Travel, 175 Fifth Ave., New York, NY 10010 (212–777–0260).

Friendly Holidays, 118–21 Queens Blvd., Forest Hills, NY 11375 (800–422–1312).

Fun Sun Tours, 7700 Edgewater Dr., Oakland, CA 94621 (800–456–6458).

Garza Tours, 14103 Riverside Dr., Sherman Oaks, CA 91423 (800–423–3178).

GoGo Tours, 120 Fulton St., New York, NY 10038 (212–385–7680).

Mexican Representatives, 3355 W. Alabama, Houston, TX 77098 (800–231–6333).

Mexico Travel Advisors (MTA), 12000 Ford Rd., Dallas, TX 25234 (800–876–4682).

TOURIST INFORMATION SERVICES. *The Mexican Government Tourist Office* at 405 Park Ave., New York, NY 10022 (212–755–7261), has only a limited amount of information and most of that is vague and generalized. Travel agents and airlines serving Yucatán airports can be much more helpful.

WHEN TO GO. High season with high prices runs from mid-December through Easter week along the Mexican Caribbean. Spring and summer usually are quite pleasant, although some rain may fall in the afternoons. Autumn is when hurricanes blow.

Within Yucatán state there are no seasonal price changes. The winter months, however, are less steamy. The hottest time is late spring just before the summer rainy season. Christmas and Easter weeks, which are unofficial Mexican holidays, may mean hotel rooms and seats on airplanes will be hard to come by.

WHAT TO TAKE. Not much will be needed, which is good news. Airlines permit passengers to check two bags and carry a bit of hand luggage on board (always carry valuable documents, essential medicine, costly cameras, and jewelry with you). Even in Mexico, however, porters are not always available and you may have to carry all your bags yourself. Best advice is to arrive with one bag packed inside another; if bargains in the shops are too much to resist, you will still be able to cart them home.

Resort wear is all that will be needed at the Caribbean playgrounds. Cancún is the most dressy spot on the peninsula, but a jacket, not to mention a tie, would be out of place. Comfortable, surefooted shoes will come in handy when clambering about the Maya ruins.

Yucatán state is a tad more conservative than the beaches. Shorts are not considered appropriate on Mérida streets, although many tourists wear them anyway. The *huipil,* an embroidered sack dress, and the *guayabera,* a tailored shirt, are favored by the locals and are as comfortable garb as one might find anywhere.

Since any hotel you are likely to stop at will have a pool, bring a swimsuit. Also bring a can or two of insect repellent.

Still, movie, and video cameras all may be brought into Mexico without hassle, along with up to 12 rolls of film for each. Kodak and Fuji dominate the market, so if you prefer another brand, bring it. When not in use, cameras should be kept locked in luggage or checked with hotel security.

Other handy items are a small flashlight, two or three ballpoint pens, a pocket calculator, a notebook, tweezers, scissors, and a sewing kit with a few spare buttons. Liquids, be they perfume or detergent, travel better in plastic bottles.

Facial tissues are perhaps the most important item. These are readily available in Mexico and usually found in hotel rooms, but are never on hand when they are most needed.

TIPS FOR BRITISH VISITORS. National Tourist Office, 60–61 Trafalgar Square, London WC2N 5DS (tel. 071–734–1058/9).

Insurance. We heartily recommend that you insure yourself to cover health and motoring mishaps, with *Europ Assistance,* 252 High St., Croydon, Surrey CR0 1NF (tel. 081–680–1234). When you need help, there is a 24-hour, seven days a week (all holidays included) telephone service staffed by multilingual personnel.

It is also wise to take out insurance to cover loss of luggage (though check that this isn't already covered in any existing home-owner's policies you may have), and also trip cancellation insurance. The *Association of British Insurers*, Aldermary House, Queen St., London, EC4N 1TT (071–248–4477) gives comprehensive advice on all aspects of vacation insurance.

Customs. Returning from Mexico you may bring home: (1) 200 cigarettes or 100 cigarillos or 50 cigars or 250 gr. of tobacco; (2) two liters of table wine and, in addition, (a) one liter of alcohol over 22% by volume (38.8° proof most spirits), or (b) two liters of alcohol under 22% by volume (fortified or sparkling wine); (3) 60 milliliters of perfume and ¼ liter of toilet water; and (4) other articles up to a value of £32.

Money Matters. It is best to provide yourself with U.S. traveler's checks or dollar bills, as they are much easier to change than European currencies.

Electricity. Usually 110 volts. You should take along an adaptor, as razor and hair-dryer sockets are usually of the American style, taking flat-pronged plugs.

Tour Operators. *Bales Tours.* Bales House, Barrington Rd., Dorking, Surrey RH4 3EJ (tel. 0306–885–991) offers a 15-day escorted tour which concentrates on archaeological sites in Central Mexico and the jungles of the Yucatán. Costs range from £1,499 to £1,745, depending on the season. Some meals are included.

Kuoni Travel, Kuoni House, Dorking, Surrey RH5 4AZ (0306–740500), has a "Mexican Panorama" tour to Mexico City, Mérida, Oaxaca, and Acapulco; 14 nights from £1,067. They also offer 7 nights in Acapulco, starting at £549.

Mexican Holidays, 23 Eccleston St., London SW1 9LX (071–730–8640) will put together a holiday for you to any part of Mexico, especially to suit your own requirements.

Voyages Jules Verne, 21 Dorset Sq., London NW1 6QG (071–486–8751), offers 15-day "Classical Tour of Mexico," which covers sites and ends with a chance to relax on the beach at Cozumel. £1,195.

WHAT IT WILL COST. The price for a holiday on the Yucatán Peninsula will depend on where you go as well as when you go and what accommodations you select. Here is what a couple might spend during a busy winter's day in Cancún:

Double room at a top hotel	$200
Breakfast, lunch, and dinner for two	100
Activities (tours, golf, sailing lessons, etc.)	65
Cocktails	20
Evening at a disco	60
	$445

Off-season the hotel room will be at least one-third less and even during the high season not all hotels charge $200. Cozumel is less costly than Cancún and Isla Mujeres is almost inexpensive. In Mérida and the rest of Yucatán state, a couple might manage to spend $200 a day, $250 if they had a rental car.

SEASONAL EVENTS. Fiesta takes on a special meaning in Maya Yucatán where celebrations are distinct from those in the rest of the country.

In addition to the traditional fiestas, there are a number of other annual fairs and shows that can add spice to a holiday.

Carnaval (Mardi Gras) takes place the week before Lent with parades, outdoor dancing, and fireworks both in Mérida and in Cozumel.

Equinox, **March** 21 and **September** 21, is when, through an interplay of light and shadow, Kukulkán, the Plumed Serpent, appears to emerge from his temple atop El Castillo Pyramid and slithers down to earth. The phenomenon attracts large crowds; be sure to make hotel reservations well in advance.

Isla Mujeres Regattas take place in late **April, May,** or early **June** as sailboats from Florida and Texas converge on the island in a series of races.

Holy Cross Fiestas start in Chumayel, Yucatán, on **April** 28 and continue until **May** 3. Cockfights, dances, fireworks, and all the rest are part of the festivities. These fiestas, however, have pagan undertones; Chumayel was a repository for ancient holy writings while Felipe Carillo Puerto—formerly known as Chan Santa Cruz—was headquarters for a Maya insurrection that lasted throughout most of the 19th century.

Hammock Festival, final week of **May** in Tecoh, on the southern outskirts of Mérida. The hammock, which originated in this part of the world, dates back to pre-Hispanic times and is preferred by many to a bed since it is cooler and insect resistent. The Hammock Festival is a fine place to check out various models and enjoy a typical fiesta at the same time.

Billfish Tournaments take place late in **May** and early **June** in Cozumel and Cancún. Dates and prizes are announced only a few months prior to the events, but information should be available from the Mexican Tourist Office (see *Tourist Information Services* above).

Fiesta of San Ignacio in Chetumal, the final week of **July.** Rather special is this festival with its reggae and calypso rhythms blending with traditional Mexican music. The nearness of Belize is never forgotten in Chetumal.

Fiesta of Our Lord of the Blisters (El Señor de las Ampollas) is Mérida's biggest. It starts **September** 27 and continues on for two weeks or more with processions, dances, bullfights, and fireworks.

Fiesta of the Christ of Sitilpech, in Izamal, near Mérida, gets started **October** 18 with a procession carrying the image of Christ from Sitilpech village to Izamal. There are daily processions with dances and fireworks for a week.

Day of the Dead, or All Saints' and All Souls' Day, is **November** 1–2 and is celebrated throughout the peninsula with graveside picnics as people herald the annual return of the departed from the spirit world.

Fiesta of Santiago, the week of November 13 in Tekax, Yucatán, features bullfights, cockfights, dancing, and fireworks.

Cancún Fair is held in November as a nostalgia trip for provincials who now live along the Caribbean shore but who still remember the small town fiestas back home.

Day of the Immaculate Conception on **December** 8 is celebrated at the fishing village of Celustún near Mérida with an impressive aquatic procession.

Circus comes to Cancún the week after Christmas, complete with big top and all the trimmings.

BUSINESS HOURS AND HOLIDAYS. In the Yucatán area shops, stores, and businesses usually are open from 10 A.M. until 2 P.M. and then from 4 until 8 P.M., closing for the midday siesta. Banks are open from

9 A.M. until 1:30 P.M. Mon. through Fri. but exchange houses keep longer hours. Most shops are open everywhere on Sat. and a few, especially in resort areas, on Sun.

National Holidays, when banks, government offices and many private businesses are closed: New Year's Day, Jan. 1; Constitution Day, Feb. 5; Benito Juárez's Birthday, Mar. 21; Labor Day, May 1; Independence Day, Sept. 16; Revolution Day, Nov. 20; Christmas Day, Dec. 25.

Semiofficial Holidays, when banks and government offices close but many private firms remain open: Holy Week, especially Thurs. and Fri. before Easter; May 5, anniversary of the Battle of Puebla; May 10, Mothers' Day; Sept. 1, opening of Congress; Oct. 12, Dia de la Raza, or Day of the Race; Nov. 2, Day of the Dead (All Souls' or Memorial Day); Dec. 12, Feast of the Virgin of Guadalupe; Christmas Week.

HOTELS. The Mexican Tourism Ministry uses a star system to classify hotels (full-length mirrors, color television, and dial phones help win five stars), and it allows maximum rates to be established accordingly. Here we consider five stars *Deluxe,* four stars *Expensive,* three stars *Moderate,* and two stars *Inexpensive* (we do not recommend one-star properties). Cancún alone in the Yucatán area boasts hotels in the "gran turismo" or *Super Deluxe* category. Hotels in beach resorts are permitted to charge more than those inland. Prices listed in this book are for a double room, European plan (without meals) unless otherwise noted. While dollar rates have remained quite stable during the past few years, they may vary somewhat by the time you read this.

DINING OUT. Good food at reasonable prices is the rule throughout most of the Yucatán Peninsula. Regional fare in Yucatán is quite distinctive from that in the rest of the country. Traditional dishes are cooked with pork, chicken, venison, and turkey.

International cuisine is available throughout the area, with pizza parlors and chow-mein salons along with hamburger heavens found from Mérida to Chetumal.

In Yucatán one dines at midafternoon and sups lightly after dark; along the coast in Quintana Roo the reverse is true with a snack at midday and a feast early in the evening the rule. Dress is casual, up to a point (the over-casual end up with tables by the kitchen door).

In Cancún, and to some extent in Cozumel, reservations are a good idea at the posher spots. Menus virtually always are printed in English as well as Spanish, but in ordering speak clearly and make certain you are understood.

TIPPING. Baffling in any foreign currency, tipping is even more confusing in Mexico. Although inflation has been reduced, the peso has steadily decreased in value at the rate of 1 peso per day. The 15% rule is fine for restaurant checks; otherwise, keep the exchange rate in mind (what, at the moment, is the equivalent of a dollar) and hand out pesos accordingly, trying not to overtip and remembering that the minimum wage is about $3 per day.

The following is a suggested tipping guide:

Bellboys—a dollar for 2–3 bags.

Porters—same as bellboys.

Maids—$1 per day.

Taxis—no tip expected, but a quarter will win a smile.

Car watchers—between a dime and a quarter, depending upon the amount of time parked and if your car is intact when you return.

Shoeshiners—no tip expected.

Service station attendents—when tires and oil are checked, windshield cleaned, a quarter; otherwise, a dime.

Tourist guides—a minimum of a dollar, $2 for a half-day tour, $3 for a full day, $20 to $25 for a week per person (more if the guide has been especially good, less if not).

Bus groups—for the driver, up to $1 per day per person.

SHOPPING. Travelers leave home to see the sights, but when they get back they talk about what they bought. Those returning from the Yucatán can babble on for hours.

Shopping specialties are listed under the various chapters in this book. Stores as a rule have fixed prices, but many small shops may be willing to negotiate. Ask if they have a discount, or what rate they give for dollars, or what the price will be if you pay in cash. At markets haggling is the rule.

Bargaining, to be sure, is an art. Probably the best results come from a sad smile and slow shaking of the head, indicating the article appeals, but is too expensive. When asked what you might pay, offer half the original price, but avoid speaking aggressively. That may win no response until you walk away. Then the battle of wits commences.

Duty-free items, especially cosmetics, are available along the Caribbean, although they seldom are bargains. Quintana Roo not so long ago was a remote territory and to some extent remains outside the pale of Mexican customs.

U.S. Customs imposes no duty on most Mexican handicrafts and is quite generous regarding tourist purchases abroad. Those who do plan big shopping sprees, however, are advised to ask for the booklet *Know Before You Go,* which spells out the latest regulations and is available from travel agents and airport customs offices. The importation of items made from animals considered endangered species is prohibited by the U.S.; Mexico prohibits the exportation of pre-Columbian artifacts and under a treaty arrangement U.S. Customs may confiscate such materials and return them to Mexico.

TIME ZONE. The Yucatán Peninsula is on Central Standard Time throughout the year. Geographically it should be on Eastern Time, but when this was tried the local folk objected; as a result the sun goes down quite early.

ELECTRIC CURRENT. All Mexico has the same 60–cycle, 120–volt system such as is used in the U.S. Power failures are not infrequent, however. Flashlights can come in handy.

CONVERTING METRIC TO U.S.
MEASUREMENTS

Multiply:	by:	to find:
Length		
millimeters (mm)	.039	inches (in)
meters (m)	3.28	feet (ft)
meters	1.09	yards (yd)
kilometers (km)	.62	miles (mi)
Area		
hectares (ha)	2.47	acres
Capacity		
liters (L)	1.06	quarts (qt)
liters	.26	gallons (gal)
liters	2.11	pints (pt)
Weight		
grams (g)	.04	ounce (oz)
kilograms (kg)	2.20	pounds (lb)
metric tons (MT)	.98	tons (t)
Power		
kilowatts (kw)	1.34	horsepower (hp)
Temperature		
degrees Celsius	9/5 (then add 32)	degrees Fahrenheit

CONVERTING U.S. TO METRIC
MEASUREMENTS

Multiply:	by:	to find:
Length		
inches (in)	25.40	millimeters (n)
feet (ft)	.30	meters (m)
yards (yd)	.91	meters
miles (mi)	1.61	kilometers (km)
Area		
acres	.40	hectares (ha)
Capacity		
pints (pt)	.47	liters (L)
quarts (qt)	.95	liters
gallons (gal)	3.79	liters
Weight		
ounces (oz)	28.35	grams (g)
pounds (lb)	.45	kilograms (kg)
tons (t)	1.11	metric tons (M)
Power		
horsepower (hp)	.75	kilowatts
Temperature		
degrees Fahrenheit	5/9 (after subtracting 32)	degrees Celsius

TELEPHONES. The most important item to bear in mind is that long-distance calls abroad are exceedingly expensive, but reasonable when made collect (this all has to do with taxes, a bit complicated to go into here). Such calls must be placed by the hotel operator and credit card calls are not always accepted. Local calls may be dialed directly from most hotels and are free.

While not on a par with the U.S., the Mexican telephone system is good. In the more remote areas of Yucatán and Quintana Roo, however, phone service may not be available.

To call Mexico from the U.S. dial 01152 and the area code (988 for Cancún and Isla Mujeres, 997 for Cozumel, 99 for Mérida).

LAUNDRY AND DRY CLEANING. Most hotels can take care of this. Budget travelers will find reasonably priced establishments even in Cancún and Cozumel, but should be certain of seeking recommendations first, since some places are worse than bad.

STUDENT/YOUTH TRAVEL. As some special facilities are available, young people who qualify should obtain an *International Student Identity Card* from the *Council on International Educational Exchange,* 205 East 42nd St., New York, NY 10017 (212–661–1414), or 312 Sutter St., San Francisco CA 94108 (415–421–3473). Canadians should contact the *Federation of Students-Services,* 171 College St., Toronto, Ont. M5T 1P7, Canada (416–977–3703).

The organizations listed below can assist in providing information on low-cost flights, educational opportunities, and other matters for young people considering travel abroad to Mexico as well as other parts of the world.

Council on International Educational Exchange (CIEE), 205 East 42nd St., New York, NY 10017 (212–661–1414), and 312 Sutter St., San Francisco, CA 94108 (415–421–3473), provides information on summer study, work–travel programs, and tours for high school and college students.

Institute of International Education, 809 United Nations Plaza, New York, NY 10017 (212–883–8200), administers scholarships and fellowships abroad, provides information on international summer educational programs and full-time programs abroad run by American institutions for academic credit.

Federation of Students-Services, 171 College St., Toronto, Ont. M5T 1P7, Canada (416–977–3703), has a travel bureau and arranges tours for students of more than 50 Canadian colleges and universities.

HINTS TO THE DISABLED. Few special facilities are offered in Mexico, but those wishing details on conditions might contact any of the following:

Society for Advancement of Travel for the Handicapped, 26 Court St., Brooklyn, NY 11242 (718–858–5483), can provide data on special tours for the handicapped and on who runs them.

Moss Rehabilitation Hospital Travel Information Service, 12th St. and Tabor Rd., Philadelphia, PA 19141 (215–329–5715), provides information on tourist sights, transportation, and accommodations around the world. The fee is $5 for each destination.

Access Tours, a travel agency specializing in travel arrangements for the handicapped, can plan tours for groups of four or more with any disability. They can be reached at Box 356, Malverne, NY 11565 (516–466–0816).

The Information Center for Individuals with Disabilities, 2743 Wormwood St., Boston MA 02210 (617–727–5540), offers useful problem-solving assistance, including lists of travel agents that specialize in tours for the disabled.

Mobility International, Box 3551, Eugene, OR 97403 (503–343–1284), has information on accommodations, organized study, etc., around the world.

HEALTH. Biggest worry is the upset stomach and diarrhea that seem to plague so many visitors to Mexico. Consulting a physician prior to departure makes sense, as does calling the hotel medic once illness strikes; this way it probably can be cleared up in hours. Tour guides and pharmacies also can be helpful in suggesting remedies. Ignored, the discomfort may last for days; self-treatment often only makes it worse.

A few other tips:

• Carry along frequently used items such as nose drops, cough syrup, and vitamins because the same brands may not be available in Mexico.

• No inoculations are required to visit Mexico, but your physician may suggest preventatives to stave off hepatitis, typhoid, or malaria.

• Bring along extra eyeglasses or contact lenses plus a copy of the prescription.

• Those who have a serious allergy or a chronic disease should wear a *medical-alert* or similar tag around the wrist or neck.

• Always carry an identification card that includes an emergency telephone number, health insurance company and policy number, and blood type.

• Keep insect repellent handy and use it liberally.

• All hotels have house physicians on call and in most cases these medics speak English. Health-care facilities in this region are good, but not great.

MAIL. Allow two weeks for cards and letters to arrive (at times they get through in a week, at other times in a month). Postage rates change without advance notice, thus making up for inflation. Post office hours are from 8 A.M. until 7 P.M. weekdays; hotel newsstands usually sell stamps, but charge a bit more than face value.

ENGLISH LANGUAGE MEDIA. *The News,* published in Mexico City, is usually available in Mérida, Cancún and Cozumel. U.S. newspapers, magazines, and books are available at hotels and shops in all three cities. Most first-class and deluxe hotels have U.S. satellite programming on their in-room television.

There are several local tourist publications in English available in the region.

CUSTOMS. As regulations, allowances, and restrictions may change at any time, it is wise to obtain last-minute information on procedures from a travel agent or the customs people themselves. Nevertheless, the following is what was prevalent at press time.

U.S. residents may bring back into the States $400 worth of foreign merchandise as gifts or for personal use without having to pay duty, provided they have been out of the country more than 48 hours and provided they have not claimed a similar exemption within the previous 30 days. Every member of a family is entitled to the same exemption, regardless of age, and the exemptions can be pooled. For the next $1,000 worth of goods a flat 10% rate is assessed.

Included in the $400 allowance for travelers over the age of 21 are one liter of alcohol, 100 non-Cuban cigars and 200 cigarettes. Only one bottle of perfume trademarked in the U.S. may be brought in. There is no duty on antiques or art over 100 years old. You may not bring home meats, fruits, plants, soil or other agricultural products.

Gifts valued at under $50 may be mailed to friends or relatives at home, but not more than one per day of receipt to any one addressee. These gifts must not include perfumes costing more than $5, tobacco or liquor.

Canada. In addition to personal effects, and over and above the regular exemption of $150 per year, the following may be brought into Canada duty-free: a maximum of 50 cigars, 200 cigarettes, 2 pounds of tobacco and 40 ounces of liquor, provided these are declared in writing to customs on arrival. Canadian customs regulations are strictly enforced; you are advised to check what your allowances are and to make sure you have kept receipts for whatever you may have brought abroad. Small gifts can be mailed and should be marked "unsolicited gift, value under $40 in Canadian funds." (You should also include the nature of the gift.) For other details ask for the Canada Customs brochure "I Declare."

DEPARTURE. A $12 airport tax is slapped on all passengers boarding international flights leaving Mexico. The tax is payable in U.S. or Mexican currency only; no traveler's checks or credit cards are accepted. Once paid, passengers clear immigration, where tourist cards are picked up.

On domestic flights a more modest airport tax is included in the ticket price. Passengers who fail to show up for a domestic flight on which space has been reserved forfeit 20% of the value of the ticket.

Passengers should arrive at the airport at least one hour prior to flight departure. Late arrivals, even those with confirmed space, may otherwise be denied boarding. Late arrivals also risk leaving without their baggage.

THE YUCATÁN PENINSULA

An Introduction

by
JIM BUDD

Jim Budd, Mexico City bureau chief for Travel Weekly, Meetings & Conventions *and* Incentive World, *has lived in the Mexican capital since 1958. A former editor of the* Mexico City News *and the Spanish-language business magazine* Expansion, *he has concentrated on travel writing for the past 15 years.*

"Our sister republic," is how many mainland Mexicans refer to the Yucatán. They smile to show they know the peninsula is not a separate country, that it only acts that way. "Our Texas," some of the more worldly call it.

There is much truth to that.

The heritage of Yucatán is Maya, not Aztec. Hernán Cortés, conqueror of Moctezuma, fled from the Maya fury. It took two generations of Montejos to bring the peninsula under Spanish rule, and even then such rule was shaky at best. And once independence had been won, Yucatán, like Texas, attempted to secede and join the United States (Washington was not interested).

That civil war, by the way, never was crushed. It dragged on for decades, fading into a somewhat uneasy truce. The rest of Mexico often seemed to try to forget about the peninsula or pretend it was not there. It has been that way for a long time.

The Mayas were the Greeks of the New World. Rather than an empire, they built city states, theocracies where a talent for art or science meant more than a talent for war. Their golden age, the classic period, lasted for most of the first millenium. About A.D. 900 it ended; scholars are still trying to figure out why.

Arrival of the Toltecs

Into this vacuum came the Toltecs who had ruled central Mexico much like the Romans ran their part of the world. Invading barbarians destroyed that empire and the Toltecs moved to establish another in Yucatán. That they did, uniting the dispirited Mayas, but only to be absorbed by them in the end. The Maya-Toltec empire lasted loosely until the coming of the Spaniards, but it was constantly racked by rebellions.

Yucatán was the first civilized area encountered by Europeans in the New World. The first expedition arrived in 1517 but found the natives unfriendly. A couple of years later Cortés tried to put in at Tulum, a city one chronicler called "grander than Seville," but was chased off. In 1527 Francisco de Montejo set out to conquer the peninsula. Twenty years later his son claimed success, although the Mérida he built on the ruins of Tiho was more of a fortress surrounded by hostile country.

Constant warring with the Spaniards destroyed what was left of ancient Maya civilization. The Indians drifted into the bush, clung to their ancient ways, and were hounded by missionaries to convert to Catholicism. Some did, some did not. Over the next three centuries, plantations—the haciendas—were set up and Mayas were lured or ensnared into working them. Most of the province, however, was untouched by European ways. Although not under the jurisdiction of the viceroy in Mexico City, Yucatán was considered so worthless that when mainland Mexico won its independence, Madrid abandoned the peninsula; the governor simply packed up and went home. Grudgingly, Yucatán agreed to become a state in the Mexican Republic.

The union proved to be an unhappy one and by 1840 Yucatán declared its own independence, which it might have won had not Mérida and Campeche started squabbling about which should be the capital. The bickering ended when Campeche became a state in its own right.

War of the Castes

All that fighting required soldiers. Maya peons were armed, which for the planters proved to be a blunder. The troops turned

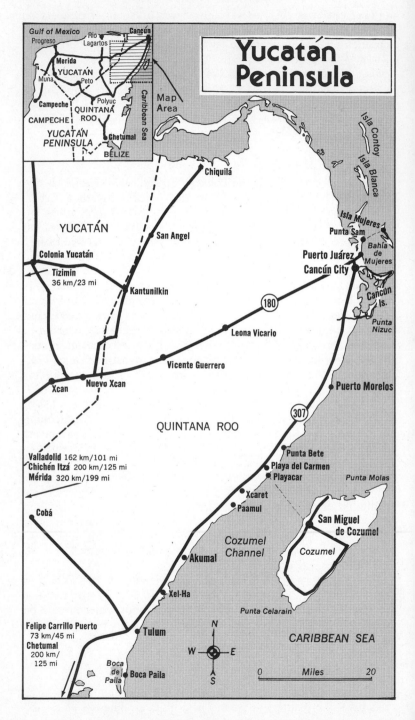

on their officers, moving to drive them out. This is when the appeal went out for annexation by the United States. It went unheeded and what is known to Mexican History as the War of the Castes blossomed.

The Mayas—the Castes (in Spanish times non-whites were categorized as castes of different grades, depending on racial mixture)—actually managed to control the eastern side of the peninsula, establishing a Maya kingdom of sorts. Battles waxed and waned, and it was not until after the outbreak of the Mexican Revolution of 1910 that peace in Yucatán more or less was restored.

In effect the Mayas won. Their kingdom was separated from Yucatán and made into the federal Territory of Quintana Roo (named, somewhat ironically, for Andrés Quintana Roo, a nineteenth-century figure who convinced Yucatán to join the Mexican Union). In effect it became an Indian reservation for Mayas.

Yucatán state, meanwhile, thrived, although only a handful of its citizens benefited. Henequen, from which twine is made, grows well on the peninsula and proved to be, as some called it, green gold. Hacienda owners became the wealthiest men in Mexico, not that they had much to do with Mexico. New Orleans, Havana, and even Paris were their meccas; neither road nor railway linked the peninsula with the mainland. Mérida flowered into a city of splendid palaces that stand today along the Paseo Montejo like haunted mansions. Eventually the Mexican Revolution with its land reforms brought in some changes, but it was the development of synthetic fibers that finally did in the old economy.

Air Age Discovery

Yet, just as the henequen buyers were abandoning Yucatán, pleasure travelers began to discover it. The ruins of the ancient Maya cities had been fascinating the world since an American wanderer, John L. Stephens, wrote about them in the mid-nineteenth century. The coming of the air age made them easy to get to.

The air age also brought new life to the Mexican Caribbean. U-boat hunters put in a strip on the once remote island of Cozumel and in their off-hours began strapping on aqualungs to probe the depths in waters some called the clearest in all creation. Once the war ended and scuba equipment turned diving into a sport, a trickle of hearty types heading for the island grew into a parade. By the 1960s, Mexicans became aware of what a treasure they had in Quintana Roo and Cancún was conceived. In 1974, the resort was born and the territory became a state.

These days Cancún gets most of the visitors who head for the peninsula. Building up the resort area was perhaps the most successful project the government ever carried out. Like Yucatán of old, Cancún is very much an entity of its own, promoting itself as a Caribbean playground and almost shunning any mention of

Mexico. Jazzy with its chrome and steel, it is one of the few places in the republic where it is safe to drink the water.

The "Other" Cancún

Actually there are two Cancúns—the swank hotel zone out along the beach (the beach is really an island connected to the mainland by a pair of bridges), and booming Cancún City. The city has mushroomed from a population of zero 20 years ago to 200,000 now. It looks it. Amazingly, Puerto Juárez next door, once the only settlement in these parts, has changed nary at all. Old-timers remember it as a few sheds and thatched huts at the end of Highway 180, the place where you boarded the ferry for Isla Mujeres. It is that way now.

Isla Mujeres is for beachcombers who like their creature comforts. None of Cancún's glamour here. Isla is the kind of place where you can show up in a tank top and cut-offs and never worry about changing clothes. Most of the hotels are in the Day's Inn category, although perhaps a bit less lavish. One gets around by bike or moped (the island is only five miles long and almost narrow enough to spit across).

Bigger than Isla Mujeres, Cozumel (30 miles long, 12 miles wide) lies just over the horizon and is where, thanks to the scuba divers, the Mexican Caribbean got its start as a resort area. Diving is still the big sport on Cozumel, giving it something of the flavor of a tropical ski town, but it also has become a favorite port of call for cruise ships, with one or two putting in almost every day.

Those who might bemoan the passing of the pristine days along Mexico's Caribbean shore need not. Highway 307, which runs south from Cancún down toward the ruins at Tulum and beyond, is dotted with roads running off to tiny isolated hotels and inns near tiny settlements like Puerto Morelos and Playa del Carmen. Along the stretch known as Akumal and farther out, communication is by radio; telephone lines have not gotten out that far.

Haven for Archaeologists

Tulum, which not too many years ago could be reached only by jeep or light plane, is currently one of the most visited archaeological zones in Mexico. Some 50 miles inland and on the shores of five small lakes are the ruins of Cobá, once a much larger center than Tulum, although now it is mostly engulfed by the jungle.

Cancún vacationers who find themselves fascinated with the area's Maya past usually, once they have seen Tulum, sign up for a day trip to the much larger and spectacular site at Chichén Itzá. Perhaps this is better than not seeing Chichén at all, but far more rewarding and less exhausting is overnighting at one of the several hotels near the ruins and then continuing on to Mérida.

Mérida is the sometimes bustling, sometimes somnambulant capital of contemporary Maya Yucatán. It is an old-fashioned kind of place with old-fashioned prices. While for most visitors Mérida is not much more than a bedroom to nap in between excursions to Chichén Itzá, Uxmal and the other archaeological zones, it is, in fact, a delightful city of attractive shops, an outstanding museum, and starry, romantic nights.

In Mérida the old ways are honored. True, along the Quintana Roo coast, hotel bellboys and maids are likely to be racially Mayan, even speaking Spanish as a second language. Culturally, however, they have been assimilated into the ways of the western world. Such, however, is not the case with many of Mérida's people.

Mayas Preserve Customs

Women are likely to wear the *huipil,* something like a sack dress embroidered at the neck and hem, and perhaps carry a silk shawl *(rebozo)* and sport a bit of gold filigree jewelry on festive occasions. Not only is such an outfit cooler and more attractive than most modern attire, but it also announces that the wearer holds to old-fashioned traditions. Maya men by custom once wore pajama-like white trousers and shirts, but in Mérida many have yielded to the temptation of cheap work pants and sport shirts.

The road to Chichén Itzá or to Uxmal passes through towns where Maya families live in single-room oval homes under a high roof of thatch, much as their ancestors did centuries ago. Such huts are depicted in sculptures at Uxmal. In these villages, the Maya gods live on beside Christian saints and the Trinity; Catholic priests may be respected, but when a miracle is needed many Mayas will turn first to the local shaman.

The fiestas in the Maya villages are wonderful, and one seems to be going on somewhere within a short drive of Mérida every week of the year. Fiestas are literally feast days when the community's patron saint is honored, often with a parade through town. There are also likely to be candlelight processions, couples dancing the traditional *jarana,* cockfights, possibly bullfights, and always fireworks, a Ferris wheel, and a carousel.

Yucatán state, then, is much more than archaeology. Mérida has its own beach at Progreso, about 20 miles north on the Gulf coast. Progreso was long something of a private preserve of Mérida's henequen princes, but nearby Yucalpetén is developing into a resort area with two new hotels open. The coast is bracketed by national parks that are preserves for great flocks of pink flamingos.

The spiky plants growing in even rows alongside the highways are henequen. Demand for natural-fiber twine declined decades ago, but production—now in the hands of the government—continues. Too few farmers know how to grow any other crop and Yucatán's porous rocky soil, watered only by occasional rain, may not be good for much else.

Henequen looks much like the century plant or *agave* from which tequila is distilled in Jalisco, mescal in Oaxaca, and from which pulque is brewed throughout much of central Mexico. The great haciendas on which henequen is grown are now communal farms. Some of the plantation homes on these onetime feudal estates have been opened as museums. Government agronomists struggle now to find alternative crops while government factories turn out rugs, carpets, and wall hangings, which, except for their bulk, make marvelous gifts.

Tourism Holds Promise

Over in Quintana Roo, another industry of old, the gathering of sap from the chico zapote tree to make chewing gum, also has been hit hard by the introduction of synthetics. No doubt the decline of chicle-gathering and henequen-growing is just as well, for those who did the work earned pennies a day and lived in misery. Tourism, the fastest-growing industry in the peninsula, holds a promise of a better standard of living.

Because it is so flat, the Yucatán Peninsula has one of the most extensive highway systems in Mexico. Cutting through miles of flat jungle, the roads are anything but scenic, but they do lead to fascinating places. From Mérida one can zip over to Felipe Carrillo Puerto, which was once Chan Santa Cruz, center of the Maya rebellion during the War of the Castes.

Chan Santa Cruz is a mixture of Maya and Spanish meaning "Little Holy Cross." Here, by a cenote or pond-like opening on an underground river, grew a tree with a cross on its trunk. The tree was said to speak with the voices of the ancient gods, urging the Mayas to fight on for their freedom. Once peace came to the area, the town was renamed for a reform-minded governor of Yucatán.

Felipe Carrillo Puerto was that governor, perhaps best remembered now for his romance with an American reporter of the 1920s. Alma Reed came to Mexico to write about the revolution, found love, and sailed back home, planning to write her stories and return for a wedding. To serenade her at dockside, Carrillo Puerto commissioned what endures as one of the loveliest of Mexican songs, *La Perigrina (The Pilgrim),* " . . . remember always my palm groves, remember always my love." Remembering, Miss Reed returned only to learn her man had been seized by his enemies and shot. She stayed on in Mexico, living out her days in the country, never marrying. She is buried by Carillo Puerto's side.

About 75 miles south of the town of Felipe Carrillo Puerto and hard by the border of Belize—once known as British Honduras—is Chetumal, capital of Quintana Roo. Someday surely a budding Graham Greene will make it the setting of a spy novel, for this odd little town close by an ancient, moated Spanish fort, lovely beaches, and inviting lagoons, seems to breathe intrigue. It lives largely on smuggling, for all of Quintana Roo is pretty much a duty-free area. Avenida Héroes is lined with shops laden with European cosmetics and Japanese electronics. Driving back to Mérida, one stops for customs inspection at the Yucatán line. It adds to the feeling that this is, indeed, a sister republic.

CANCÚN

Mexico's Caribbean Resort

by
JIM BUDD

Fable has it that Cancún was discovered by computer. Like most fables, this one requires some suspension of disbelief. It scarcely seems possible that it took an electronic brain to decide to develop this bit of heaven, a 12-mile-long strip of talcum sand washed by the gentle turquoise Caribbean and backed by the most romantic of jungle lagoons.

As far as it goes, it scarcely seems possible that Cancún has not been luring in vacationers for as long as planes have been flying and ships sailing. Yet the first hotels opened only in 1974.

The story is told of how in the 1960s, with the birth of the jet age, Mexico woke up to the tremendous possibilities tourism offered. Acapulco was booming and more Acapulcos were needed. Bankers and bureaucrats scoured the country, fed their findings into data processors, and came up with Cancún.

Some had their doubts. In those days Cancún was a remote jungle-covered sand bar that seemed to be a million miles from nowhere. There was no electricity, no telephone lines, no potable water, and no way to get there.

Constructing all that needed infrastructure appeared to be an enormous gamble. Instead it turned out to be about the most successful project the Mexican Government has ever undertaken. The only problem with Cancún today is that there are not enough rooms to meet demand. The construction goes on.

In reality there are two Cancúns. One is the hotel zone on the beach along an island almost narrow enough to spit across. The other is Cancún City on the mainland, home for 200,000 people, the fastest growing community in the country.

Elegant Hotel Zone

The hotel zone is all elegance and luxury. It has been built up following a master plan that bans the garish and ugly. There are no gaudy signs out this way and nothing trashy or tacky is allowed. The plans for every structure are carefully studied by the powers that be and nothing unappealing is approved.

With the sea on one side and the lagoon on the other, just about every hotel room on the island looks out on the water. Kukulkán Boulevard, which extends the length of the island, is the zone's single avenue. Hotels and condo complexes (the condos outnumber the hotels) are for the most part none too close to each other. Except for the area around the Convention Center, the Hotel Zone is not a place for strolling. (At press time part of the Convention Center was operating, but the Anthropology Museum was almost totally destroyed by Hurricane Gilbert and is being rebuilt.)

This might be called the center of town, or at least of the island. Several of the finest hotels are clustered in this neighborhood, along with restaurants, discos, and both elegant shopping malls and a sort of flea market, one of the few reminders that this still is Mexico.

One almost always approaches Cancún from the south, driving in from the international airport on the mainland, passing through the scrub jungle and on across the little bridge that leads onto the island.

Contrasting Views

Out this way, one catches a glimpse of Cancún the way it once was—scraggly, ragged, far from charming. Then construction cranes are seen in the distance. The first condos are spotted, along with signs announcing where glamorous new hotels are to be erected. Next come the pleasure palaces already built.

Vacationers putter along on mopeds or electrically powered surreys. The Caribbean comes into view, breathtaking in its beauty. The lagoon is off on the left, half-hidden, the way it would be in an old Tarzan movie; then it opens to the broad expanse of water where water skiers and jet skiers dart about.

Kukulkan Boulevard continues beyond the Convention Center, past the high rises and the low rises, the malls, the boutiques, the

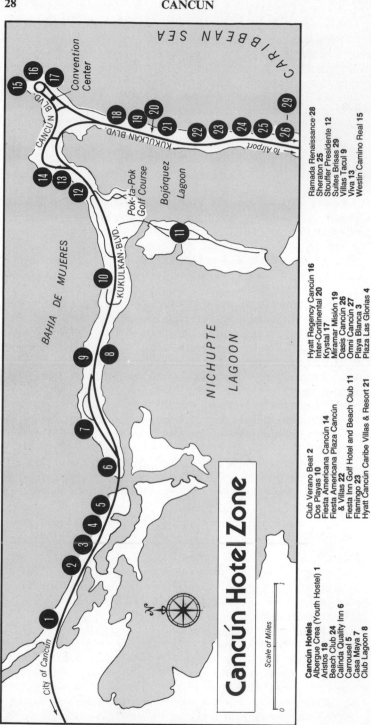

Cancún Hotel Zone

CARIBBEAN SEA

BAHIA DE MUJERES

NICHUPTE LAGOON

Convention Center

CANCÚN BLVD.

KUKULKAN BLVD.

KUKULKAN BLVD.

Pok-ta-Pok Golf Course

Bojórquez Lagoon

City of Cancún

To Airport

Scale of Miles

Cancún Hotels
Albergue Crea (Youth Hostel) 1
Aristos 18
Beach Club 24
Calinda Quality Inn 6
Carrousel 5
Casa Maya 7
Club Lagoon 8

Club Verano Beat 2
Dos Playas 10
Fiesta Americana Cancún 14
Fiesta Americana Plaza Cancún & Villas 22
Fiesta Inn Golf Hotel and Beach Club 11
Flamingo 23
Hyatt Cancún Caribe Villas & Resort 21

Hyatt Regency Cancún 16
Inter-Continental 20
Krystal 17
Miramar Misión 19
Oasis Cancún 26
Omni Cancún 27
Playa Blanca 3
Plaza Las Glorias 4

Ramada Renaissance 28
Sheraton 25
Stouffer Presidente 12
Suites Brisas 29
Villas Tacul 9
Viva 13
Westin Camino Real 15

restaurants and discos, until it eventually makes its way onto another bridge and into Cancún City.

Cancún City

Like the hotel zone, Cancún City was built according to a master plan. Unlike the hotel zone, ugliness was not banned. The city looks like the boom town it is: raffish and roaring, home for the busboys and chambermaids, the porters and taxi drivers who make the hotel zone work.

Almost everyone who stays on the island makes at least one excursion into the city; budget travelers often stay at its inexpensive hotels and bus themselves out to the beaches every day. Bus service in Cancún is quite good, with fares the equivalent of a quarter or so.

Shopping and eating are the joys of Cancún City. Tulum is the main drag, with many good restaurants along the side streets running into Tulum. These side streets are large U's, each encircling a block and maintaining the same name; thus as one wanders along Tulum, one crosses Claveles, for example, and continuing along crosses it again. Cancún City has its curious features.

Puerto Juárez Unchanged

A couple of miles north of the city is Puerto Juárez, once the only settlement in these parts and remarkably unchanged for all the progress that has gone on around it. A ferry to Isla Mujeres departs from Puerto Juárez.

Off in the other direction is the highway that leads to the Maya ruins at Tulum, 80 miles away.

Along with visiting Cancún City, almost everyone vacationing in Cancún makes a day trip to Isla Mujeres and makes another to Tulum. Dedicated Maya buffs can also head to the more spectacular ruins at Chichén Itzá and be back in a day, but this can be an exhausting trip.

In some ways it is surprising that anyone who gets to Cancún would be willing to leave, even for a few hours. Yet one of the secrets of Cancún's success is that there is so much to do.

EXPLORING CANCÚN

The beaches, of course, are the big attraction. Hurricane Gilbert in 1988 rearranged the beaches considerably, but sand was brought in to bring them back to normal. Those busing in from the city can choose any beach they like; the seashore in Mexico is federal property and available to anyone who wants to use it. Lonesome stretches, how-ever, should be avoided when it comes to swim-

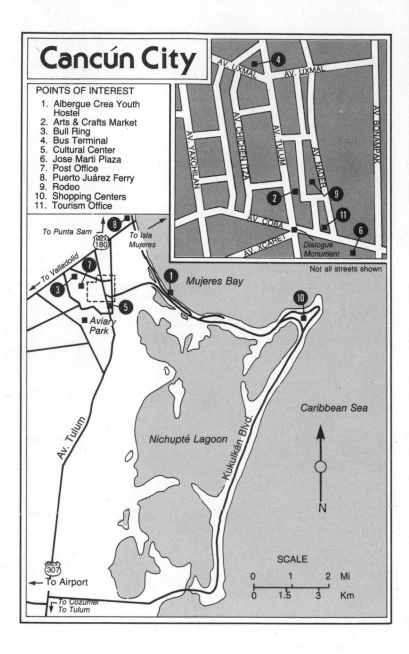

Cancún City

POINTS OF INTEREST

1. Albergue Crea Youth Hostel
2. Arts & Crafts Market
3. Bull Ring
4. Bus Terminal
5. Cultural Center
6. Jose Marti Plaza
7. Post Office
8. Puerto Juárez Ferry
9. Rodeo
10. Shopping Centers
11. Tourism Office

Not all streets shown

AV. UXMAL
AV. UXMAL
AV. YAXCHILAN
AV. CHICHEN ITZA
AV. TULUM
AV. NADER
AV. BONAMPAK
AV. COBA
AV. XCAHET
Dialogue Monument

To Punta Sam
To Isla Mujeres
To Valladolid
MEX 180
Mujeres Bay
Aviary Park
Av. Tulum
Nichupté Lagoon
Kukulkán Blvd.
Caribbean Sea
N
MEX 307
To Airport
To Cozumel
To Tulum

SCALE

0	1	2	Mi
0	1.5	3	Km

ming. The undertow in Cancún can be dangerous; almost all the hotels have lifeguards on duty.

The sun, naturally, is another major attraction, and it, too, should be treated with caution. Cancún boasts more sunny days than almost any other Caribbean destination, but there always is the temptation to get started too quickly on a tan for fear it may be cloudy tomorrow. Clearly this is not a good idea, as a bad burn can ruin a holiday.

The big beach sport is para-sailing, soaring in a parachute pulled by a speedboat. It is thrilling and not quite as dangerous as it looks, but accidents do happen.

Sailing, windsurfing, waterskiing, jet skiing, and snorkeling all can be arranged at most beachfront hotel sports centers or at any of the many marinas that dot the island. Instructors are available to show how it is done. The tranquil waters of the lagoon are ideal for mastering these skills.

Paradise for Divers

Scuba diving is at its best along the Mexican Caribbean. The waters are both warm and astoundingly clear (in many areas of the world divers must don rubber suits to keep from freezing and once below the surface consider themselves lucky if they can see 20 feet in front of them). For novices, resort courses are available as well as certification courses; these latter take several days to complete.

Deep-sea fishing off Cancún may not be as spectacular as off Baja California, but in many ways it can be more fun. The crews, for instance, can arrange to put in at Contoy or one of the other small islands and fry up the catch for a picnic. As for billfish, late spring is the best time to go after them.

The big sport on shore is golf at Pok-Ta-Pok (the Maya phrase for ball game) where the 18-hole course was designed by Robert Trent Jones. The course, quite frankly, has been trouble-plagued since it was laid out, first by flooding, later by winds, and most recently by plant diseases that did in both grass and palms. It remains, nevertheless, a grand challenge as well as a chance to see both the lagoon and the sea from a different vista. It is also the only golf course in the world that includes the ruins of a small Maya temple among its hazards.

Pok-Ta-Pok's facilities include a practice green, a club house, and a pro shop where electric carts and pull carts as well as clubs and shoes may be rented. Caddy service is available, as is instruction. There are also tennis courts on the premises.

Most of the island hotels have tennis courts and most of them are lit for play after dark.

Getting Around

Taxis are the easiest way of getting around the island and fares are quite reasonable. Bus service, as mentioned, is quite good and at least one trip should be considered as part of the Cancún experience. Vacationers staying at one of the hotels near the Convention Center are pretty much within walking distance of the malls, the flea market, and many of the restaurants on the island. Getting into town requires wheels; most folks don't go into town until the cool of the evening.

Those who don't golf, play tennis, fish, waterski, or scuba will probably spend the first day or two in Cancún by the pool or on the beach simply unwinding. A couple may opt for breakfast in bed (which beats waiting in line for the buffet), order a snack for lunch, go out some place splendid for dinner, and continue on to a disco.

Evenings start early in Cancún, possibly because the sun sets so soon (as mentioned, Cancún should be in the Eastern Time Zone; that was tried but the locals resisted) and possibly because American vacationers outnumber the Mexicans and Americans prefer not to wait around until 9 P.M. for dinner. Be that as it may, the action starts at dusk with happy hours in the lobby bars.

The choice of restaurants is nearly as wide as in Mexico City itself. Everything from tacos and chow mein to blackened redfish and wienerschnitzel is available. The hotels on the island strive to outdo each other and the independent beaneries struggle to be the best of all.

Mainland More Funky

At least one evening should be spent over on the mainland in Cancún City. The restaurants in town tend to be a bit more funky and relaxed than the elegant spots on the island, and usually are a bit less expensive. Dress, even at the best places on the island, is casual. A man in a jacket and tie would feel somewhat out of place. Shorts, jeans, and bare feet, on the other hand, are a tad too informal.

Nighttime entertainment centers around the discos and lobby bars, along with moonlight cruises and weekly Mexican fiestas at various hotels. Extra special is the Folkloric Ballet at the Convention Center each evening; a buffet dinner can be combined with a show that highlights the regional dancing of Mexico. If the Anthropology Museum has been rebuilt, part of an evening should also be set aside to see a reenactment of the Equinox Light and Sound Show at the replica of Chichén Itzá's El Castillo Pyramid.

The equinox phenomenon is little less than astounding. El Castillo Pyramid was built to honor Kukulkán, the Plumed Serpent God whom the Mayas worshipped as the font of almost every blessing.

A temple to the diety tops the pyramid while a carved snakehead rests on the ground at the base of a balustrade. On March 21 and September 21—the days of the equinox, planting time and harvest time—shadows strike the balustrade in such a way that Kukulkán appears to be slithering out of his temple and down the side of the pyramid to fertilize the earth. How this happens is demonstrated twice each evening at the mock-up by the Convention Center.

Cancún also has its bullfights and charro rodeos. Bullfights are held year round with the bulls charging out on Wednesdays at 3:30 P.M. instead of the traditional 4 P.M. on Sundays. The charro rodeos are more sporadic, but great fun if you can catch one. Both men and women participate, the ladies demonstrating their riding skills while the males go in for rope tricks and literally throwing the bulls. Hotel travel desks have details on when these shows take place.

Day Cruises

Cruises over to Isla Mujeres are probably the biggest selling item at hotel travel desks. Both sailing catamarans and motor yachts make the trip. Either way, getting there and back is half the fun (those prone to seasickness might not agree). The boats put in at El Garrafón, an underwater park where the snorkeling is sensational. Some trips include lunch, others allow time for a meal at one of the many pleasant restaurants on shore.

A cheaper alternative is to take the public ferry over to the island. Boats usually leave every couple of hours but it is best to arrive fairly early, for once a ferry has its full compliment of passengers, off it goes. It also is wise not to plan on taking the last boat back in the evening as there may be no room on board.

A car-and-passenger ferry leaves from Punta Sam at about two-hour intervals from 7 A.M. to 10 P.M. There is also a water taxi that transports passengers only for about $5. The majority of the ferries leave from Puerto Juárez, a couple of miles from downtown Cancún. You can get there by bus or taxi. Puerto Juárez not so long ago was the only settlement on this stretch of Mexico's Caribbean coast and it still has much of the flavor of that vanished era.

These boats, which make the crossing in less than an hour and charge about 50 cents for passage, put in at the one little village of Isla Mujeres. Quaint is what it is, a handful of inexpensive hotels, pleasant restaurants, and tiny shops. The adventurous will want to hire a moped to explore the island, perhaps riding out to El Garrafón where snorkeling equipment is available for rental.

Another fascinating boat trip is aboard a catamaran waterjet that runs over to Cozumel in about 30 minutes. Being aboard this vessel is like being aboard a wide-body jet, complete with an in-transit movie. One can spend the day on that island and return on the catamaran or fly back to Cancún in a light plane that is nothing at all like a jet.

Bus Tours of Ruins

A favorite excursion is a bus tour to the Maya ruins at Tulum some eighty miles south of Cancún. Tulum is unique both for being the only walled city known to have been built by the Mayas as well as the only settlement constructed right on the coast. While archaeologists consider this post-classic community with some disdain, the setting by the beach with what appears to have been a castle overlooking the cliffs is spectacular.

The Tulum tours usually include a stop for snorkeling at Xel-Ha (shell-ha), lagoons where fresh water blends with the sea. This is a national park and a natural aquarium where snorkeling is at its best.

Chichén Itzá, more than 100 miles west of Cancún, is a more tiring one-day trip, with buses arriving when the heat of the day is at its worst and scarcely allowing trippers to see even a fraction of the site. Still, this is one of the great archaeological zones of the world, and there are those who feel a quick glimpse is better than seeing nothing at all.

Cancún itself has its own ancient ruins including the remains of tiny temples on the grounds of the Camino Real and the Sheraton as well as a small ceremonial center, further out on the island, known as El Rey, which means "the king." Skeletons were found here and there is some speculation this may have been a princely burial ground.

Mopeds, which are little scooters, are a fun way of getting around Cancún, although the saddles may be a little rough on the tailbone. They also can be a trifle dangerous for any rider taking a spill. There are, at least, special paths that usually keep these bikes out of the traffic lanes, but accidents do occur, and in Cancún there is nobody to sue.

Rental cars are a safer bet. There are more than a dozen car rental firms in Cancún, but most of the available vehicles are un-air-conditioned, standard-shift subcompacts. Big luxurious cars should be reserved in advance.

Rental cars are fun for those who want to get away from Cancún to explore the Caribbean coast, perhaps heading up to the ruins at Cobá beyond Tulum or driving down all the way to Chetumal and maybe crossing the border into Belize (be certain to obtain written authorization from the rental firm and to bring along travel documents). With a rental car, one can overnight at one of the hotels near Chichén Itzá or even swing up to Mérida, capital of Yucatán.

Beware of Peddlers

Most people, however, once they land in Cancún, never want to leave. True, as with any resort, there are those who love Cancún and those who hate it. Detractors scorn its lack of charm, its newness and artificiality. Perhaps its worst feature is the swarm of condominium peddlers who pester anyone they can stop with invitations to free breakfasts, orgies, or what-have-you in return for listening to some spiel about the joys of time-sharing.

The best testimonial in favor of Cancún is its popularity. Those who enjoy resort vacations return year after year. Hotels always seem to be full and only a gambler will take a chance of arriving without a confirmed reservation in his pocket. The computer that discovered this once-hidden heaven scored a bull's-eye.

PRACTICAL INFORMATION FOR CANCÚN

HOW TO GET THERE. Most international travelers arrive by air. By road Cancún is perhaps 30 driving hours from the U.S. border and for those who have the time it can be an enjoyable trip. There are some coach tours which take in the entire Gulf Coast and the archaeology of Tabasco, Chiapas, Campeche, and Yucatán, winding up on the Caribbean with an option of returning home by air. Regular buses will appeal only to the adventurous or the penniless.

By Plane. Packages that include air fare and hotel are usually the most economical way to travel. Best bargains are the VTI and VTP packages sold only within Mexico by *Mexicana* and *Aeroméxico;* these include some ground arrangements and offer discounts of up to 40%. On international routes, all airlines usually charge the same, but often there are special promotional deals and excursion tariffs.

Aeroméxico flies nonstop from Houston and Campeche; *American* from Dallas/Fort Worth; *Continental* from Houston; *Eastern* from Miami; *Lacsa* from New Orleans; *Mexicana* from Baltimore/Washington, Chicago, Dallas/Fort Worth, Los Angeles, Miami, Philadelphia, and Tampa as well as from several points within Mexico; *Northwest* from Memphis; and *United* from Chicago.

By Car. Those driving from the U.S. will probably follow the Gulf Coast Highway from McAllen or Brownsville; Route 101 joins 180 which runs all the way to Cancún. This is an excellent way to see the country, although the scarcity of unleaded gasoline in Mexico may be a worry. Roads are two-lane blacktop in fair to good condition and patroled by the Green Angels, who provide mechanical assistance when needed. Driving after dark should be avoided. Good hotel accommodations are available all along the route.

By Bus. Travel agents have information on motorcoach tours that take in the Gulf Coast and the Maya country, winding up in Yucatán. Most of these are operated only in the winter months, departing from points near the Texas border. Regular bus travel is good enough, although far from luxurious. Confusion is the major problem for passengers, especially those who do not speak Spanish.

TELEPHONES. Area code for Cancún is 988; to call from the U.S. first dial 01152. Within Cancún long-distance calls usually must be made through the hotel operator and because of taxes, collect calls are much less expensive.

The number for the U.S. Consulate Office in Cancún is 4 2411; for the tourist office, 3 0208.

HOTELS. New is a relative term in Cancún, which didn't exist before 1974. All hotels in Cancún are "new"; most were built within the past 10 years. The pace of hotel construction has quickened in the past few years, with resorts planned or going up on virtually every lot on the hotel strip. Cancún can also boast of more *Super Deluxe* ($180–$230) resorts than any other spot in Mexico; *Deluxe*, $150–$180; *Expensive*, $100–$150; *Moderate*, $60–$100; *Inexpensive*, under $60. Rates are for the winter season; they drop by at least one-third between May 1 and December 15. All Cancún Island hotels are located on the Cancún Hotel Zone map.

Super Deluxe

Hyatt Cancún Caribe Villas & Resort. Kukulkán Blvd.; Cancún Island; 3 0044 or, in U.S., 800–228–9000. Cozy, with 198 rooms and 20 beachfront villas, pool, tennis, restaurant, and nightly entertainment.

Fiesta Americana Cancún. Kukulkán Blvd., Cancún Island; 3 1400 or, in U.S., 800–223–2332. Built to resemble a village encircling a swimming pool, a resort with 281 terraced rooms where the emphasis is on fun at 3 restaurants; plenty of evening entertainment.

Hyatt Regency Cancún. Kukulkán Blvd., Cancún Island; 3 0966 or, in U.S., 800–228–9000. A distinctive 12-story circular high-rise with a striking atrium and 300 rooms including 8 suites and 25 Regency Club rooms, all with balconies. Three restaurants, several bars, and nightly entertainment.

Krystal. Kukulkán Blvd., Cancún Island; 3 1133 or, in U.S., 800–231–9860. Run by a leading Mexican chain, Krystal has 318 rooms and suites, large pool, all water sports, outstanding restaurants, and a spectacular discotheque.

Sheraton. Kukulkán Blvd., Cancún Island; 3 1988 or, in U.S., 800–325–3535. Off by itself with 725 rooms and suites in 4 adjoining buildings, 4 pools, 6 lighted tennis courts, miniature golf, 4 restaurants, and a discotheque.

Westin Camino Real. Kukulkán Blvd., Cancún Island; 3 0100 or, in U.S., 800–228–3000. A Cancún classic with 381 rooms and 28 suites, all with individual terraces and a sea view, large pool, artificial lagoon, all water sports, and 3 lighted tennis courts. A new tower with 87 rooms was opened in July 1989.

Villas Tacul. Kukulkán Blvd., Cancún Island; 3 0000. An exclusive complex of 2- to 5-bedroom villas, most of them on the beach. All services.

Deluxe

Beach Club. Kukulkán Blvd., Cancún Island; 3 1177. An all-suites establishment with 157 units (all with kitchenettes and cable TV) out on an empty stretch of beach. Two restaurants, 3 bars, tennis, and shops.

Inter-Continental. Kukulkán Blvd., Cancún Island; 5 0755 or, in U.S., 800–332–4246. A resort complex with 261 rooms, 2 lighted tennis courts, pools, a health club, water sports, restaurant, and coffee shop. A portion of the beach has been restored following Hurricane Gilbert.

Omni Cancún. Kukulkán Blvd., Cancún Island; 5 0184 or, in U.S., 800–THE–OMNI. This new hotel has 281 deluxe rooms, 33 suites, 14 beachfront villas, and 2 presidential suites, each with a large terrace. There are 3 restaurants, a lounge, 3 lighted tennis courts, a health center, a pool, and a rather narrow beach.

Ramada Renaissance. Kukulkán Blvd., Cancún Island; 5 0100. On the west end of the island at Playa del Rey, this pyramid-shaped hotel has 223 rooms, 3 suites, an Olympic-size pool, restaurant, coffee shop, and lobby bar.

Expensive

Calinda Quality Inn. Kukulkán Blvd., Cancún Island; 3 1600 or, in U.S., 800–228–5151/52. Somewhat spartan are the 460 rooms, not all of which look out on the sea, but the beach is one of the best on the island; the pool is nice and there is a restaurant plus 2 bars.

Carrousel. Kukulkán Blvd., Cancún Island; 3 0513. Another low-cost beachfront hotel with 149 terraced rooms overlooking the Caribbean. The bar is a local favorite.

Casa Maya. Kukulkán Blvd., Cancún Island; 3 0555 or, in U.S., 800–221–6509. A hotel with 100 rooms and 250 suites, 2 pools, tennis courts, and a variety of evening entertainment.

Club Lagoon. Kukulkán Blvd., Cancún Island; 3 1111. A bungalow complex on, as the name implies, the lagoon, with 70 rooms, 19 duplex suites, a marina, and all water sports, plus a charming restaurant.

Fiesta Americana Cancún. Kukulkán Blvd., Cancún Island; 3 1400 or, in U.S., 800–223–2332. Built to resemble a village encircling a swimming pool, a resort with 281 terraced rooms where the emphasis is on fun at 3 restaurants; plenty of evening entertainment.

Fiesta Americana Villas Plaza Cancún. Kukulkán Blvd., Cancún Island; 3 1022 or, in U.S., 800–223–2332. A complex of 56 beachfront villas containing 100 suites, managed by the prestigious Fiesta Americana group.

Fiesta Inn Golf Hotel and Beach Club. Paseo Pok-Ta-Pok, Cancún Island; 3 2200. The location makes sense for golfers as it's right next to Cancún's only golf course. The small, but attractive 2-story hotel has 120 rooms, an inviting pool area, restaurant, coffee shop, and lobby bar.

Flamingo. Kukulkán Blvd., Cancún Island; 3 1544 or, in U.S., 800–922–7866. Somewhat isolated, with 162 nicely furnished rooms and suites, large pool, Jacuzzi, pleasant beach, several shops.

Miramar Misión. Kukulkán Blvd., Cancún Island; 3 1755. Flagship of a growing Mexican chain with 255 rooms and suites, pool and beach, three restaurants, and nightly entertainment.

Oasis Cancún. Kukulkán Blvd., Cancún Island; 5 0867. This sprawling hotel has 1,000 rooms and suites in several pyramid-shaped structures in lush gardens. There are 11 bars and restaurants, an open-air amphitheater on a private lake, a ¼-mile-long swimming pool, 4 tennis courts, and health club.

Stouffer Presidente. Kukulkán Blvd., Cancún Island; 3 0200 or, in U.S., 800–472–2427. Since its renovation, completed in spring 1988, this 293-room property is one of Cancún's best. The location is excellent, especially for golfers. There are 2 pools, tennis courts, and evening entertainment.

Suites Brisas. Kukulkán Blvd., Cancún Island; 5 0302. This 203-suite property has a delicatessen and Continental restaurant, pool, and tennis.

Moderate

America. Avenida Tulum, Cancún City; 4 1500. One of the best downtown hotels with 180 large, terraced rooms, pool, and free shuttle service to hotel's own beach club.

Aristos. Kukulkán Blvd., Cancún Island; 3 0011 or, in U.S., 800–223–0888. One of the first beachfront hotels with 222 rooms, tennis, pool, and all water sports.

Club Verano Beat. Kukulkán Blvd., Cancún Island; 3 0722. A small (77-room) condo hotel with pool, tennis court, restaurant, and a popular disco.

Hotel América. Tulúm and Brisas Aves., Cancún City; 4 1500. A centrally located, pleasant hotel that welcomes families, the América has 180 air-conditioned rooms and free shuttle bus service to the beach. There's a good size pool, restaurant, bar, and coffee shop.

María de Lourdes. Avenida Yaxchilan 1537; 4 1721. This popular resting spot for travelers from around the world has 51 rooms, a restaurant, nightclub, and pool.

Playa Blanca. Kukulkán Blvd., Cancún Island; 3 0344 or, in U.S., 800–528–1234. One of the pioneer hotels on the island, close to town, a 161-room Best Western with a marina, tennis court, and restaurant.

Plaza Las Glorias. Kukulkán Blvd., Cancún Island; 3 0811. On the beach with 110 rooms, 2 restaurants, and a bar. Close to town.

Viva. Kukulkán Blvd., Cancún Island; 3 0019 or, in U.S., 800–421–0767. Well-run, with 210 rooms overlooking a tranquil beach. Pleasant piano bar.

Inexpensive

Albergue Crea. Kukulkán Blvd., Cancún Island; 3 1337. A beachfront government-run hostel for youths of all ages, with cable TV, pool, and dormitory beds. The largest installation of its kind in the country.

Antillano. Tulum at Claveles, Cancún City; 4 1132. In the busiest part of downtown, with 48 air-conditioned rooms and a bar.

Batab. Avenida Chichén Itzá 52, Cancún City; 4 3822. More of a commercial hotel for business travelers, this 68-room inn has air-conditioning and a restaurant.

Cotty. Avenida Uxmal 44, Cancún City; 4 1319. A nicely run air-conditioned inn, but still little more than a place to sleep at night.

Dos Playas. Kukulkán Blvd., Cancún Island; 3 0500. Small and well-run, with 107 rooms pool, a tennis court, and good restaurants.

Handall. Tulum at Jaleb, Cancún City; 4 1122. A motel that is ugly on the outside but has passable rooms and a tiny pool.

Plaza Caribe. Tulum at Uxmal, Cancún City; 4 1377. With 140 rooms, this is one of the larger downtown hotels and it features a big pool, restaurant, coffee shop, and lobby bar.

Soberanis. Cobá near Tulum, Cancún City; 4 1858. The 65 rooms are squeaky clean if none too attractive. Known more as a restaurant than as a hotel.

Villas Maya Cancun. Avenida Uxmal 20, Cancún City; 4 1762. A small complex with 14 rooms in a residential area; nice for those who want to stay for 2 or 3 weeks.

DINING OUT. Along with the sun, the sand, and the sea, restaurants are among Cancún's top attractions. Hotels make a strong effort to keep guests on the premises, but in these pages we list only truly exceptional hotel food outlets while attempting comprehensive coverage of the independently operated cafes. The choice is wide, both on the island and in the city. The basic price for a meal will run $25 and up in a *Deluxe* establishment, $15–$25 in an *Expensive* place, $10–$15 in a *Moderate* restaurant, and below $10 at an *Inexpensive* spot. These prices include a 15% sales tax, which may be itemized to help you figure the tip (be sure to check the check). Drinks will be extra, and quite a bit extra if the booze is imported. Dinner, the big meal of the day in Cancún, usually is served anytime from 7 P.M. until 10 P.M. and maybe later. Reservations, especially at *Deluxe* and *Expensive* restaurants, are a good idea. Credit cards are abbreviated as AE, American Express; MC, MasterCard; and V, Visa.

Deluxe

Beefeater's. Across from the Convention Center, Cancún Island; 3 0693. Open from noon to midnight, featuring hearty fare, a big salad bar, and large drinks. Fun. AE, MC, V.

Blue Bayou. At the Hyatt Caribe, Kukulkán Blvd. Cancún Island; 3 0044. Cajun and New Orleans cooking (there is a difference) served in a lush tropical setting by a lagoon. AE, MC, V.

Bogart's. Across from the Convention Center, Cancún Island; 3 1133. Right out of the movies, Cancún's answer to *Rick's Cafe Americaine* in *Casablanca,* with an even better menu. Reservations suggested. AE, MC, V.

El Mortero. Across from the Convention Center, Cancún Island; 3 1133. A full-scale replica of a hacienda plantation home with a menu featuring Mexican gourmet country cooking. Reservations suggested. AE, MC, V.

Mauna Loa. Kukulkán Blvd., Cancún Island; 3 0693. A bit of the South Seas on the Caribbean serving Szechuan and Mandarin as well as Polynesian specialties. Shows nightly at 7 and 9. Reservations suggested. AE, MC, V.

Maxime. Kukulkán Blvd., Cancún Island; 3 0438. Quite chic with superb decor, a dignified setting, and an interesting Continental menu. Reservations suggested. AE, MC, V.

Expensive

Bombay Bicycle Club. Kukulkán Blvd., Cancún Island; 3 1698. As wacky as the name sounds, fairly close to town and open for breakfast and lunch as well as dinner. MC, V.

Carlos 'n Charlie's. Kukulkán Blvd., Cancún Island; 3 0846. The local link in an international chain of fun spots with good food. AE, MC, V.

Chac-Mool. Kukulkán Blvd., next to the Aristos hotel, Cancún Island; 3 1107. The name is Mayan but the food is Continental, the music classical, and the atmosphere romantic. AE, MC, V.

El Campanario. Avenida Tulum at Cobá, Cancún City; 4 4180. Good Mexican food served in a fine Mexican setting with entertainment nightly. Open 8 A.M. to midnight. Reservations suggested. MC, V.

Gypsy's Pampered Pirate. Kukulkán Blvd., Cancún Island; 3 2015. Something of a fisherman's shack built on stilts over the lagoon, with good steaks and super seafood. Flamenco show every night at 7:30 and 9:30. Open for breakfast, lunch, and dinner. MC, V.

La Dolce Vita. Avenida Cobá 87, Downtown; 4 1384. Indoor or outdoor dining; excellent Italian specialties and homemade pasta. AE, MC, V.

La Habichuela. Margaritas 25, Cancún City; 4 3129. Where the local elite meet to eat. Open from 1 P.M. to midnight. Reservations suggested. MC, V.

Moderate

Augustus Caesar. Claveles 13, Cancún City; 4 1261. An Italian place, complete with checkered tablecloths, good for scaloppine and fettucine. MC, V.

Casa Salsa. Kukulkán Blvd., Cancún Island; 3 1114. Lively atmosphere. Specialties are grilled meats and seafood. Mariachi music 6–11 P.M. AE, MC, V.

Fonda del Angel. Avenida Cobá 85, Cancún City; 4 3393. Mexican specialties plus lobster and steak served at lunch and dinner, indoors and outdoors. MC, V.

Karl's Keller. Plaza Caracol Mall, Cancún Island; 3 1104. German cooking where sausage and strudel is served with a Teutonic flare. MC, V.

Peacock Grill. Hotel Plaza Caribe, Cancún City; 4 1377. Hearty fare includes lobster and prime rib at attractive prices. MC, V.

Pepe's. Kukulkán Blvd., Cancún Island; 3 0835. Everything from ribs to lobster, plus a popular bar. Casual and fun. MC, V.

Inexpensive

Almendros. Tulum at Sayil, Cancún City; 4 0807. While not fancy, this branch of Mérida's most popular eating place is highly recommended for its Yucatán regional specialties. AE, MC, V.

Augustus Pizza. Convention Center, Cancún Island; 3 0530. An outdoor spot, open for breakfast as well as lunch and supper.

Pop. Avenida Tulum 26, Cancún City; 4 1991. Open for breakfast and on until 10 P.M. and next to City Hall, this is where the local politicos gather.

Rolandi. Cobá 12, Cancún City; 4 4047. Pasta at its best, along with pizza, served up in a garden setting. AE, MC, V.

Selva Negra Deli. Plaza Quetzal, Cancún Island; no phone. A European-style delicatessen with German pastries, cold cuts, and wines.

Super Deli. Tulum, Cancún City; 4 1122. Pizzas, sandwiches, hamburgers are served all day and all night. MC, V.

HOW TO GET AROUND. Transportation of some sort often will be needed as both the island and Cancún City are fairly spread out. Happily, bus service is good and taxis inexpensive.

Airport Transfers. Perhaps the most uncomfortable ride in town is aboard the minibuses that have a monopoly on transferring passengers from the airport either to the island or into town. Rates, at least, are reasonable (about $2 per person) with tickets sold in the arrivals area. Dollars may be changed into pesos at the airport at favorable bank rates.

Buses. These vehicles run from outlying hotels all along Kukulkán Blvd. past the Convention Center and into Cancún City. If not luxurious, they are fun and the fare is less than a quarter.

Taxis. Cabs are found outside most hotels as well as cruising; rates are posted at hotel entrances and in Cancún cabbies seldom cheat, although word has it that they aren't as honest as they used to be. Tipping is not customary.

Rental Vehicles. While hardly a necessity except for exploring outlying areas, rental cars are available at the airport or from any of a dozen agencies, including those with international names. Most of these autos are standard-shift subcompacts and jeeps; air-conditioned cars with automatic transmission should be reserved in advance. Rental cars are expensive in Cancún, as everywhere in Mexico.

Large, late-model air-conditioned cars (the next best thing to limousines, which are unavailable in Cancún) with English-speaking chauffeur may be hired through hotel travel desks.

Mopeds and scooters are available outside the Hotel Krystal and at several other island locations. While fun, these are risky and no insurance covers accident victims. Electrically powered surreys, for daytime use only, may be rented at Plaza Caracol on the island for $15 per hour.

Ferries. Boats leave Puerto Juárez (just outside Cancún City) for Isla Mujeres every couple of hours, but schedules are flexible; fare is about half-a-dollar. A catamaran waterjet departs for Cozumel from Playa del Carmen every two hours or so from 4A.M. to 7:30 P.M.; a one-way ticket costs about $2.

TOURIST INFORMATION. *Cancún Tips,* a pocketsize booklet, is available in most hotel rooms and is on sale around town; a handy guide, it does, however, limit listings to advertisers. The publishers also maintain an information office by the Convention Center and at the Convention Center (El Parián), Plaza Caracol, and Royal Marina; open weekdays 8 A.M.–8 P.M.; Sat. 9 A.M.–1 P.M., and Sun. 10 A.M.–8 P.M. The State Tourist Department has a booth at the airport and several others scattered about the island; these are staffed 9 A.M.–1 P.M. and 5–9 P.M. daily except Sun.

TOURS. Picnic cruises to Isla Mujeres and excursions to Maya ruins are favorite tours.

Several vessels head over to Isla Mujeres. The *Don Diego* and *Don Diego II* trimarans (3 0606) sail daily from the marina at the Playa Blanca Hotel. The 6½-hour trip costs $25 and includes snorkeling at Isla Mujeres' Garrafón Beach, drinks, lunch, and—for those who volunteer—swinging on the spinnaker. *Aqua-quin* (3 0100), also a trimaran, makes a similar voyage for $32 from the marina at the Westin Camino Real. *El Corsario* (3 0200), a 50-foot motor sloop, heads for Isla Mujeres from the marina at El Presidente Hotel, and while there is no spinnaker to swing from, the vessel is more steady. The price is $29. *Fiesta Maya* (3 1804), a large motor launch, sails from its pier in the lagoon and on to Isla Mujeres. The boat's glass bottom allows nonsnorkelers to view marine life and there is a dance band on board, but the $28 fare includes Continental breakfast, open bar, lunch on the beach, and fiesta on board. *El Tropical Treasure Island* leaves Cancún Island at 8 A.M., charges $30, and includes a shopping stop at Isla Mujeres, two hours at El Garrafón for snorkeling, and a buffet lunch at *Villa Pirata. Columbus* (3 1488) offers a dinner sail on the lagoon from 4:30 to 7:30 P.M., including a lobster or steak dinner and open bar for $45.

Evenings there is a "Pirates' Night" cruise on the *El Tropical* (3 1488) geared toward singles (and those who wish they were). The 6 P.M. cruise includes a buffet and show for $33.

Cesna airplanes are available for trips to Cozumel, Chichén Itzá, and other sights in the surrounding area. For charter information, contact Pelican Pier Avioturismo (3 0315, 3 1935). For $40 it will take you on a 15-minute flight over Cancún in an ultralight seaplane that takes off from the lagoon.

Coach tours to the Maya ruins at Tulum take the better part of a day and include snorkeling stops at Xel-Ha Lagoon. The ruins themselves are only 80 miles from Cancún; they are by a beach and are small enough to be easily seen in a short time. Several agencies run these tours and most charge about $20.

Coach tours to Chichén Itzá, more than 100 miles distant, cost about $25 and can be exhausting. Dedicated sightseers, however, will not want to miss what is truly one of the grandest of the ancient ceremonial centers. Lunch is included in the trip.

Cozumel tours, round-trip by bus and jetfoil cost about $45, with lunch and sightseeing included. Cozumel is the original resort island in the Mexican Caribbean, charming in many ways, but on a one-day visit there really is not very much to do except stroll about the village, eat, and wait to head back to Cancún.

Landlubbers can get a view of the depths of the sea from the keels of the catamaran *Nautilus* which leaves from the San Marino dock at 10 A.M., noon, and 2 P.M. for a 1½ hour tour (3 1004 or 3 2119).

Most people book these tours through their hotel travel desks. Arrangements can be made directly, however, by calling any of the following tour operators: *Avisa,* 4 0238; *Cancun Holidays,* 5 1515 or 3 0161; *Ceiba Tours,* 4 1962; *Expreso Mexicano,* 4 1456 or 3 0044; *Mayaventuras,* 4 2244; *Moreno Travel,* 3 0747; *Rutas del Mayab,* 3 1504; *Visusa,* 4 3095.

BEACHES. Cancún Island is, of course, one long beach, although various stretches have individual names. By law all the seashore, which is federal property, is open to the public. Two areas, Tortuga Beach and Chac Mool, have restaurants and changing areas which make them especially nice for vacationers staying at the beachless Cancún City hotels. Overall, the beaches on the stretch of the island closest to the city are best for swimming; farther out the undertow can be tricky. Most hotels have lifeguards, but drownings do happen. Stick to the pool when red warning flags fly by the sea and avoid swimming off lonely stretches of beach.

BABY-SITTING SERVICES/CHILDREN'S ACTIVITIES. Almost all hotels can arrange for a baby-sitter on a few hours' notice. These sitters, however, may not speak any English. During the summer months many Mexican families vacation in Cancún. Hotels often arrange for special activities and many have shallow pools for the younger set.

PARTICIPANT SPORTS. Water sports of all kinds are big in Cancún, everything from deep-sea fishing to scuba diving. There is para-sailing, windsurfing, jet-skiing, waterskiing, snorkeling, and sailing, and most of the hotels on the island have their own sports activity centers. In addition there are several marinas about the island including *Playa Blanca* (3 0606), *Club Lagoon* (3 1011), *Aqua Tours* (3 0400), and *Wild Goat Marina* (3 0062), which has jet skis. *Scuba Cancún* (3 0315) specializes, as the name implies, in diving trips. *Avioturismo* (3 0315) operates a large fishing fleet.

Deep-sea **fishing** boats and other gear may be chartered from the outfits mentioned above for $330–$500 per day, depending on the size and equipment of the vessel as well as the season and demand. A 2-tank **scuba dive** costs about $50 and a resort course in using scuba gear about $79. **Snorkeling** gear is rented from $8–$10 per day. **Windsurfers** are available for $14 per hour; 3 hours of lessons in how to windsurf can run from $40–$50. **Hobie Cats** rent for $35 per hour or $45 with an instructor. **Waterskiing** costs $30 for 30 minutes and **para-sailing** $20 for 10 minutes.

Golf is played at Pok-Ta-Pok, Kukulkán Blvd. (3 0871), a private club where the 18-hole course was designed by Robert Trent Jones. Caddies, electric carts, and pull carts are available at the pro shop and lessons can be arranged. The club has a practice green, swimming pool, tennis courts, and a restaurant.

Many hotels have **tennis** courts which can be illuminated for play in the cool of the evening. (See *Hotels* section above.)

SPECTATOR SPORTS. Bullfights are held year-round at the ring outside Cancún City on most Wed. afternoons starting at 3:30. Tickets, available at hotel travel desks, cost $25 for 3 bulls. **Charro rodeos** are held periodically. Again, hotels have full details.

HISTORIC SITES. El Rey is a minor Maya ruin near the lagoon on Cancún Island. As skeletons were found there, it may have been a regal burying ground. It is not very impressive, appealing only to those who want to say they have seen a Maya ruin and then get back on the beach. Both the Sheraton and Westin Camino Real boast the remains of small Maya temples on their premises.

MUSEUM AND GALLERIES. The *Anthropology Museum* (3 0688) at the Convention Center, virtually destroyed in 1988 by Hurricane Gilbert, was still in the process of being rebuilt at press time. If reopened, it is a good introduction to the area's Mayan past and small enough to see in less than an hour. Artifacts, including masks, sculptures, jewelry, and pottery, are on display. While labeling is in Spanish, English-speaking staffers are eager to provide explanations and answer questions.

Orbe (3 1333) in the Plaza Caracol Mall specializes in sculptures and paintings by contemporary Mexican artists; *La Galeria* is both the salesroom and studio of Gilberto Silva in the Costa Blanca Mall; *Las Palmeras* (3 1415), also at Costa Blanca, and *Akakena* (3 0539), by the Convention Center, display replicas of Maya art, temple rubbings plus contemporary painting and sculpture.

SHOPPING. Stores on master-planned Cancún Island are either in hotels or shopping malls. In downtown Cancún City, they are along the streets. Rents being lower in the city, prices should be, too, but that is not always the case. One is advised to shop carefully and favor reputable-looking establishments; "Let the buyer beware" is a philosophy with some sleazy merchants.

Resort wear and handicrafts are the best buys in Cancún. Handicrafts include a tremendous range of goods, everything from blown glass and hand-woven textiles to leather and jewelry. On the island, *El Caracol* (3 1038), with some 50 outlets, is the largest mall. Others are *El Quetzal* (no phone), *Plaza Flamingo* (no phone), *Costa Blanca* (3 0244), *Plaza Nautilus*

(3 1114), and the outdoor market, *El Parian* (3 0203), by the Convention Center.

In Cancún City *Plaza Mexico* on Avenida Tulum has 50 shops specializing in Mexican handicrafts, most of these stores concentrating on the output of a single state or region. Avenida Tulum is the main shopping street downtown.

SHOWS. The *Folkloric Ballet* dinner show at the Convention Center is an especially pleasant way to spend an evening. Performed are stylized versions of Mexico's regional dances, including the famous hat dance and the bamba. The buffet prior to the show is a sampling of Mexican regional cooking. Price for everything is about $30. For information and reservations, call 3 0199.

NIGHTLIFE. Where do you go after cocktails during a lobby bar happy hour or a long, leisurely dinner? In Cancún the choice is wide.

Discos. *Aquarius,* Westin Camino Real, Cancún Island (3 0100), prides itself on being subdued and elegant. *Christine,* Hotel Krystal, Cancún Island (3 1133), is the most spectacular disco in Mexico and the most popular in Cancún. *La Boom,* Kukulkán Blvd., Cancún Island (3 1458), is not always quite so crowded. *Mine Company,* Club Verano Beat, Cancún Island (3 0722), is Cancún's first disco and long a favorite with the locals.

Live Music. *Casa Salsa,* Caracol Mall, Cancún Island (3 1114). Live mariachi music nightly. *Batachá,* Hotel Miramar Mision, Cancún Island (3 1755). A piano bar with a bit of a dance floor. *Friday López,* Hotel Fiesta Americana, Cancún Island (3 1400). Two bands, ribs and such to eat; a favorite with singles. *La Palapa,* Club Lagoon Hotel, Cancún Island (3 1111). Romantic, indeed seductive, on a pier over the lagoon; drinks and dancing. *Hyatt Cancún Caribe*, Kukulkán Blvd., Cancún City (3 0044). Drinking and dancing in the Cassis Lobby Bar. *Reflejos,* Hyatt Regency, Cancún Island (3 0966). A chic lounge with a small dance floor. *Gifrey's*, upstairs from *L'Alternative*, Avenida Bomapak, Cancún City (4 1229), for a quiet evening in elegant surroundings. There is a *Mexican Fiesta* almost every evening at one of the island resorts with dance groups, mariachis, and fireworks.

MÉRIDA

Capital City of Yucatán

by
JANE ONSTOTT

Jane Onstott, who writes, translates, and edits educational materials, has worked and traveled extensively in Mexico, Central America, and Spain.

Though labeled the White City and the City of Windmills, Mérida nevertheless defies categorizing—it is distinctly Mexican and yet it's not at all typical. A stroll down the once-glamorous Paseo Montejo reveals the no-longer-dazzling white paint of earlier, more prosperous years, and the windmills that once supplied water from the peninsula's complex system of underground cisterns have been replaced with modern pumps.

But Mérida has the close-knit, friendly allure of a small town with the amenities of a larger, more cosmopolitan capital city. It was among the first cities built on the continent, yet it was allowed to languish unattended by the rest of Mexico until the reconstruction of ruins and the building of Cancún drew attention to the area. Even during the extremely prosperous days of the henequen boom, Mérida was thought of as a kind of outpost of civilization.

Mérida is all too often used strictly as a base from which to visit the nearby archaeological sites. Travelers who leave the city at dawn to tour the ruins, returning exhausted in the evening, will miss out on Mérida's casual charm. It's a much better idea to stay overnight in one of the hotels at the ruins—both Uxmal and Chichén Itzá have a few comfortable hotels surrounded by jungle. Enjoy a full day's sight-seeing at the ruins, and in the evening float contentedly in the hotel pool, and enjoy dinner and drinks in the restaurant. Look at a million stars and, maybe, see an owl or a really large and colorful iguana. You'll appreciate the ruins more that way, and perhaps have a few days in Mérida to shop and see a folkloric ballet or an evening of free entertainment in one of the city's pleasant parks.

Proud Yucatecos

While Cancún is chrome and glass with its hoteliers and restaurateurs imported from elsewhere in Mexico, Mérida is faded pastels with most of its inhabitants having lived there for generations. Méridians are unpretentious, yet rather proud of their unique status among the newcomers to the Mexican republic. One definitely gets the feeling that these smiling city-dwellers are Yucatecos first; Mexicanos, second.

The capital of the State of Yucatán, Mérida embodies a blend of Maya and colonial traditions, with a dash of the Middle East and Europe thrown in for subtle seasoning. The machismo of the Mexican male is noticably, exquisitely absent. The university draws scholars and the atmosphere is one of quiet culture. An added bonus is that people here think in pesos, not dollars, which always adds up to more of a vacation bargain.

Mérida is built on the ruins of the Mayan city of T'hó, or Tihó. The *zócalo,* or main plaza (officially called the Plaza de la Independencia), is located on the base of the Temple of H-Chum-caan. T'hó was one of the last Maya strongholds against the Spanish. After the defeat of the Mayas, the powerful Montejo family renamed the ruined city Mérida, for the city in southern Spain.

The Montejo family palace still stands on the south side of the *zócalo,* a monument to the family who literally made Mérida. The bas-relief on the facade of the great home, built in 1550, depicts Francisco de Montejo (the younger), his wife and daughter, and, in addition, Spanish soldiers standing on the heads of the vanquished Mayas. This arrangement is interesting since it parallels the Mayas' own habit of depicting themselves standing on the heads of defeated foes.

Legend of a Statue

Mérida's main plaza is a charming one; S-shaped *confidentes* (benches designed to facilitate "confidential" chats) are shaded by

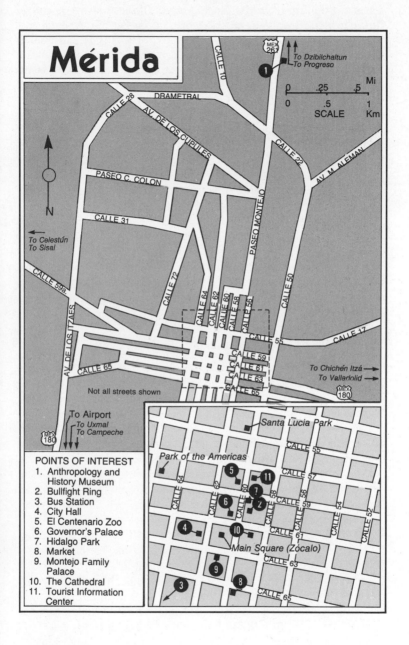

Mérida

CALLE 10
DRAMETRAL
CALLE 28
AV. DE LOS CUPULES
PASEO C. COLON
CALLE 31
CALLE 22
AV. M. ALEMAN
PASEO MONTEJO
CALLE 50
CALLE 59a
CALLE 72
CALLE 64
CALLE 62
CALLE 60
CALLE 58
CALLE 56
CALLE 55
CALLE 17
AV. DE LOS ITZAES
CALLE 65
CALLE 59
CALLE 61
CALLE 63
CALLE 65

To Dzibilchaltun
To Progreso

MEX 261

Mi
0 .25 .5
0 .5 1
SCALE Km

N

To Celestún
To Sisal

To Chichén Itzá →
To Valladolid →

MEX 180

Not all streets shown

To Airport
To Uxmal
To Campeche

MEX 180

Santa Lucia Park
Park of the Americas
CALLE 55
CALLE 57
CALLE 59
CALLE 61
CALLE 63
CALLE 65
CALLE 64
CALLE 62
CALLE 60
CALLE 58
CALLE 56
CALLE 54
CALLE 52
Main Square (Zócalo)

POINTS OF INTEREST
1. Anthropology and History Museum
2. Bullfight Ring
3. Bus Station
4. City Hall
5. El Centenario Zoo
6. Governor's Palace
7. Hidalgo Park
8. Market
9. Montejo Family Palace
10. The Cathedral
11. Tourist Information Center

century-old laurel trees, some of which are manicured in geometric
designs. Look up from the plaza and you'll see the twin spires of
the yellow cathedral—impressive for its size if not for its architec-
tural splendor. Built in 1561, the cathedral was indeed designed
for defense, and looks more like an impenetrable fort than anything
else. Without, it is stark and unadorned, with gunnery slits instead
of windows; inside, it is rather bleak, having been ransacked during
the days of the Mexican Revolution and never restored. The loot-
ers, however, did not touch the Christ of the Blisters (El Cristo
de las Ampollas). Legend has it that a peasant saw a tree burning
all night, yet in the morning, it was untouched by the effects of
fire. A statue of Christ was carved from the wood of that tree, and
placed in a church in the town of Ichmul. Later the church burned
down, but the statue survived, although burned and covered with
blisters. It was relocated in Mérida's cathedral.

On the northeast side of the zócalo is the Palacio de Gobierno
(Governor's Palace), notable for the murals depicting the history
of the Yucatán, painted by the well-known Fernando Castro
Pacheco. The arcaded Palacio Municipal (City Hall), across from
the cathedral, dates from the Montejo era. Its original function was
that of jail as well as city hall; it was reconstructed along colonial
lines in 1928.

Influence of Land Barons

Another impressive edifice is the Teatro Peón Contreras. This
theater of neoclassic design was completed in 1905 by Italian artists
imported for the task by Mérida's wealthy land barons. The first
Yucatecans to successfully exploit the area's resources were ex-
porters of dyewood (also called logwood), which was at the time
much valued in Europe. After interest in dyewood waned, henequen (or sisal) from which twine and rope are made, as well as chicle, the natural base for chewing gum, became the sources of local
wealth. The rich landowners built with their profits the lovely mansions that line Paseo Montejo, as well as the Peón Contreras Theater and other public works.

Imported goods were shipped to Mérida from Europe, filling
fashionable homes with Italian tiles, Carrara marble, and the an-
tique furniture that can still be seen in many homes. Other hold-
overs from the town's financial zenith include horse-drawn carriages, called calesas. During World War II, henequen was largely
replaced by synthetics on the world market, and chicle has since
suffered the same fate. Land barons lost the base of their wealth,
and the decline is evident in the once-stunning mansions, some of
which have been remodeled to fill other functions. These mansions
are still stately and impressive, however, and give Mérida an Old
World appearance, at least along the Paseo Montejo.

A Walking Tour

Mérida is a fabulous town for walking around and just looking. Many of the buildings were constructed in the colonial style, although having been built after Mexico gained its independence, they are not truly colonial. Around the plaza are cafes, restaurants, juice bars, and small shops.

The market is a fun place to wander, even when you're not in the mood to buy. A kind of culture indicator, the *mercado* is the place to absorb and inhale and see Mexico: a bundle of pungent-smelling herbs; whole plucked chickens and skinned rabbits; an entire alleyway of gladiolas, calla lilies, and tuberoses; carefully stacked arrangements of tropical fruits.

In Mérida the marketplace, having no clearly marked boundaries, spills out into the street in the form of stalls and small stores. *Comedores,* simple eateries that generally feature one or two inexpensive specials each day, are squeezed between stores selling fabulous treasures and those offering the ubiquitious, brightly colored plastics.

There are a lot of things to buy in Mérida, in government-run shops (where fair prices are marked and there's no need to barter), museum shops, and privately owned stores, as well as at the market. The hammocks from this region are famous throughout Mexico, and beyond; the *guayabera* shirts manufactured here are worn by men—from waiters to governors—in every Mexican city and village. There are many straw and palm products to buy, such as purses, mats, baskets and bags; leather sandals and jackets; embroidered *huipiles* (the sacklike dresses worn by local women); and exotic liqueurs.

Plazas Are Pleasant

When you're tired of shopping or walking, you can sit on a bench in one of Mérida's many plazas. There are more than a few small, cheerful plazas sprinkled around downtown Mérida, each with its own raison d'être.

Parque Hidalgo (officially named Cepeda Peraza, but no one calls it that), one block up from the *zócalo,* is a popular meeting place. There are restaurants with outdoor dining, a bookstore, and a cinema. Taxis and horse-drawn carriages wait here for customers. You can get your shoes shined, read the paper, nibble nuts purchased from a vendor, or simply sit and relax.

In the tiny Plaza de la Madre, a pretty white representation of the Madonna and Child catches the eye. It seems as if almost before you get tired, you'll find another small park in which to cool your heels.

The Yucatán Peninsula is a glorious place, and the distance between archaeological treasures (there are at least 200 ruin sites on the peninsula), a pristine coastline, coral reefs, colonial cathedrals, and *cenotes* is comfortably small. Mérida is connected to these places of interest by a series of good state and federal highways, making possible a vacation combining cultural enrichment and beach-combing, snorkeling, or scuba diving with shopping and good dining.

The important and impressive ruins of Uxmal as well as the smaller sites at Sayil, Labná, Kabah, and others are part of the *puuc* (hill) country south of Mérida. In this area are also a few small towns of historic significance, such as Mani, the once-important center of Mayan culture. Here Bishop Diego de Landa burned all but three surviving Mayan codices, books, and documents in an attempt to rout the devil from the still-unconquered peninsula. Also on this loop of highway is Ticul, a hammock and pottery center worth seeing if you're in the area. You can visit these ruins and towns on your own or on an organized tour—either way you may choose to make it a day trip or spend the night in Uxmal. The illuminated grottoes of Loltun, between Labná and Mani, contain beautiful stalactites and stalagmites, and examples of petroglyphs and wall paintings. The area south of Mérida is spotted with *cenotes,* or sinkholes, filled from Merida's vast underground system of rivers—excursions can be arranged through travel agents in Mérida.

Towns of Hammocks and Pyramids

There are many interesting sites en route to other destinations throughout the peninsula. Going east toward Chichén Itzá, Valladolid, and Cancún, for example, you can detour on Highway 80 to pass through Tixkokob, another hammock town. Farther on you'll pass Izamal, painted yellow since the days of colonial decree, and the site of a large pyramid, partially reclaimed by the tenacious scrub of the peninsula. Even more impressive than the pyramid is the enormous church and convent of Saint Anthony of Padua, with its imposing atrium, built by the Franciscan monks on the remains of pyramid Popolchac—the highlight of Izamal's dilapidated downtown.

Along the way you'll pass *cenotes* in which you can swim, such as Xtojil, about 12 miles west of Chichén Itzá, and underground caves such as those at Balancanchén, where you'll see gigantic stalagmites and underground pools. On the western coast of the peninsula, hunters stalk the small jungle deer, wild boar, jaguar, wild turkey, quail, and duck.

Mérida is a convenient base for archaeology enthusiasts, swimmers, divers, hunters, and those interested in practicing their Spanish or their Mayan. The region has a distinctive cuisine, quite different from other Mexican states, and you will want to explore some of these regional dishes as well, and sample the three fine beers brewed on the peninsula, and the sweet honey liqueur, Xtabentún, considered the nectar of choice of the Mayan gods.

PRACTICAL INFORMATION FOR MÉRIDA

HOW TO GET THERE. Mérida is located at the top of the Yucatán Peninsula, which is edged by the Gulf of Mexico on the west and northwest, and the Caribbean on the east. Most international travelers visit Mérida on their way to or from Cancún, Cozumel, or Isla Mujeres, or as an overnight side trip from one of the islands. The road trip from Mexico City to Mérida takes about 25 hours. Bus tours are a good way to see and visit many interesting sites along the way. Regular buses and trains are available, but they take longer and appeal most to those who refer to themselves as travelers rather than tourists.

By Air. Nonstop flights to Mérida are available from Miami, Mexico City, Cancún, Cozumel, and Villahermosa. Connections are made in Mexico City from many cities in the U.S.; it's about a 90-minute flight from Mexico City via *Aeroméxico* or *Mexicana*. From the airport, it's only about 4 miles to downtown Mérida. Vans provide transportation to hotels for about $3 for up to 4 passengers. If you're driving to downtown Mérida from the airport, turn right (north) onto Highway 261. Turn right onto Calle 59, just past Parque del Centenario. Calle 59 will take you downtown, right to the *zócalo* (main square).

By Bus. Mérida can be reached from anywhere in Mexico, via first- or second-class bus. In first class you are assigned, and therefore assured, a seat. Second-class traveling is recommended only for those who consider people packed together, sometimes with animals for market, to be an important part of the travel experience. Bus travel is extremely inexpensive, and the difference in price between first and second class is almost nothing. The main bus station is at Calle 69 #544 between Calles 68 and 70 (24 9263). Buses leave for Chichén Itzá, Valladolid, and Cancún every hour, 6 A.M.–noon. Buses leave frequently for Uxmal, Kabah, and Tulúm, and at 8 A.M. for Cobá. Buses to many other peninsular locations depart from here as well. Buses to Progreso, Dzibilchaltúm, and the northern coast leave from the station at Calle 62 #524, between Calles 65 and 67 (24 8991). To reach Celestun, Sisal, or Oxkutzcab, go to Autotransportes del Sur, Calle 77 #541-C (24 9675).

By Train. Rail service to Mérida is not recommended, but for those who want to try it the station is about half-mile northeast of the *zócalo* on Calle 55 between Calles 46 and 48 (23 5944). There are two trains daily to Campeche and one a day (leaving at 4 P.M.) to Valladolid. Both trips take about 4 hours and one-way fares are under a dollar. There is a daily train to Mexico City; the trip supposedly takes 36 hours, but often there are delays. No first-class service is available. A second-class ticket is less than $7. At press time sleeping-car service was unavailable.

By Car. Traveling by car is a good way to enjoy the Yucatán's scenery, and it enables you to take side trips which might seem to be a hassle under other circumstances. Reservations through such well-known companies as *Hertz, Avis, Thrifty,* and *Budget* can be made in advance by your travel agent. You can pick up the rental car at the airport, or in downtown Mérida. From Mexico City, it's about 1,000 miles to Mérida, and the roads are good. Allow 4 days to enjoy all the places in between.

If you rent a car in Cancún, it's a direct drive west along Hwy. 180 to Mérida. You'll pass through Valladolid, Chichén Itzá, and lots of tiny little towns along the way. From Campeche, it's about a 2-hour drive to Mérida up Hwy. 180. Or take Hwy. 261 from Campeche, which goes past the site of the ruins at Uxmal, as well as other interesting Mayan villages; about a 2½-hour drive. From Chetumal it's probably most efficient to take Hwy. 307 to Felipe Carrillo Puerto, then Hwy. 184 to Muna, continuing north on Hwy. 261. These paved highways are all fairly new and still in good shape. Major highways are patrolled by Green Angels (see *Tips to the Motorist* section in *Facts at Your Fingertips* chapter).

TELEPHONES. The area code for Mérida is 99. Long-distance calls can be made from the *casetas de larga distancia* in the Edificio Condesa, Calle 59 between Calles 62 and 64. Open daily 8 A.M.–11 P.M.; no charge for collect calls. Others are located at Santa Lucia Park and the main bus station, and in the northwest quarter at Calle Reforma and Avenida Colon (closed for lunch 1–5 P.M.), and Calle 57 #449 (8 A.M.–10 P.M.). Calling from one's hotel is the simplest option, if that service is available. Don't forget to call collect when making international calls from within Mexico; it's about 60% cheaper than dialing direct. (From a pay phone you must call collect.)

Pay telephones cost 100 pesos. If you plan to make many calls from pay phones, have a cache of 100-peso coins; they aren't widely circulated and you may find yourself with none. Dial 09 for the international operator (they speak English); 02 for the domestic operator (will probably speak only Spanish); and 04 for local information.

The following Mérida exchanges may come in handy: *State Tourism Office,* there will almost always be someone who speaks English (24 9495 or 24 5655); *U.S. Consul* (25 5011); *Swiss Consul* (23 9033); *Dutch Consul* (21 6850); *British Consul* (21 6799). In an emergency, call the police, who generally speak only Spanish (25 2555), or the *Red Cross,* medical emergency (21 2445); for non-emergency, call 21 6813. For 24–hour ambulance service, call 23 8711 or 21 3056.

ACCOMMODATIONS. Hotels in Mérida reflect the essence of the city itself: charming and charismatic, with an air of making the modern world fit into an old-fashioned setting. Most hotels here are built around a central courtyard or garden where a profusion of Mérida's tropical plants grow together in ordered chaos. As is true all over Mexico, the facade of the building rarely reveals the character of the hotel behind it, so check out the courtyard of a hotel before turning away unimpressed or disgruntled. Most hotels are located either downtown or on or near Paseo Montejo, which is lined with slightly dilapidated yet beautiful mansions. Downtown is more convenient for those given to spontaneous ramblings and curio collecting. All first-class and moderate rooms have air-conditioning. The rating system given here is for high season, Dec. 15–Apr.; off-season rates usually drop off by about one-third. *Deluxe,* about $75; *Expensive,* $40–$50; *Moderate,* $25–$40; *Inexpensive,* under $25.

Deluxe

Holiday Inn. Avenida Colon #498 at Paseo Montejo; 25 6877 or toll free in U.S. 800–465–4329. This large hotel has 214 rooms with televisions and telephones, restaurant, bar, discotheque, swimming pool, laundry service, travel agency.

Expensive

Hotel los Aluxes. Calle 60 #444 near Calle 49, uptown; 24 2199; in U.S., 800–221–6509 or from New York 800–522–0457. A new, modern hotel with all the amenities. Outdoor cafe, fancy restaurant, swimming pool and sundeck. Parking lot.

Hotel Casa del Balam. Calle 60 #488, 2 blocks north of *zócalo;* 24 8241 or 24 8844. A charming older hotel of neocolonial design, with 54 rooms surrounding a pretty courtyard. Restaurant, pool, bar, travel agency, group facilities.

Hotel El Castellano. Calle 57 #513, 1½ blocks northwest of main plaza; 23 0100. This high-rise hotel has 170 comfortable rooms, restaurant, bar, pool, cocktail lounge.

Hotel María del Carmen. Calle 63 #550, 5 blocks west of *zócalo;* 23 9133. Newer hotel with 94 carpeted rooms. Large pool, restaurant, shops, free parking. Now affiliated with Best Western.

Hotel Calinda Panamericana. Calle 59 #455, 4½ blocks northeast of *zócalo;* 23 9111. An elegant older hotel combining charm and comfort. Now a Quality Inn. Large pool, open-air restaurant, folkloric shows in evenings.

Misión Merida. Calle 60 #491, 2 blocks north of *zócalo;* 23 9500. A long-time tourist favorite, recently refurbished. 147 rooms. Small pool, 2 restaurants (one with glassed-in patio), bar with music nightly; folkloric shows.

Montejo Palace. Paseo Montejo #483; 24 7644. An 8-story edifice with 90 rooms, most with balconies. Rooftop nightclub, sidewalk cafe, pool, restaurant, travel agency.

Moderate

Autel 59. Calle 59 #546, 4 blocks northwest of main plaza; 24 2100. Modern hotel designed for comfort, not charm. Room music, television, mini-bars. Restaurant, cocktail lounge, pool.

Gran Hotel. Calle 60 #496, on Parque Hidalgo; 24 7622. This Victorian-looking hotel has high, painted ceilings and other elaborate touches. Large rooms surround a well-kept central garden. Nice location, but may be noisy.

Hotel Caribe. Rincón del Parque Hidalgo #500, downtown; 24 9022. A delightful hotel, with a good location on a pretty square. 60 rooms with wood paneling and music. Small pool, nice restaurant and bar.

Hotel Colón. Calle 62 #483, 1½ blocks north of *zócalo;* 23 4355. A really quaint, colonial-style hotel with 53 rooms, restaurant, bar, pool, steam rooms.

Hotel Colonial. Calle 62 #476, downtown; 23 6444. Old, but well-maintained hotel with 73 air-conditioned rooms. Pool, bar, nice restaurant.

Hotel del Gobernador. Calle 59 #535, downtown; 23 7133. A new hotel with a small pool. Most of the 59 rooms have balconies. Restaurant, bar, travel agency.

Hotel Paseo de Montejo. Paseo Montejo #482; 23 9033. The 92 rooms have televisions and mini-bars. Garden, sidewalk cafe, swimming pool, bar.

Inexpensive

Hotel Centenario. Calle 84 #498; 23 2532. A 33-room inn in a residential area for those who want to get away from other tourists.

Hotel Dolores Alba. Calle 63 #464, 3½ blocks east of *zócalo;* 21 3745. A friendly hotel with parking in central courtyard, small pool, breakfast served in dining room. Some rooms air-conditioned.

Hotel Mucuy. Calle 57 #481, 3 blocks northeast of *zócalo;* 21 1037. 23 rooms surrounding a pleasant garden, 2–3 beds per room. No air-conditioning.

Hotel del Parque. Calle 60 #495, 1½ blocks north of *zócalo;* 24 7844. A small hotel, with 20 rooms, some of which are air-conditioned. Television rental, parking.

Hotel San Luis. Calle 61 #534, near downtown; 24 7588. 40 rooms, most are air-conditioned. Pool, restaurant.

Trailer Park

Rainbow Trailer Park. 5 miles north of the city on the highway to Progreso. 60 full-service hookups, laundry, bathrooms, showers. Small unfiltered pool.

DINING OUT. Yucatécan cuisine is distinctive, foreign even to many Mexicans. Although the Yucatán is surrounded on three sides by the sea, Yucatécan dishes do not highlight seafood, but it is widely available. Traditional dishes are cooked with pork, chicken, venison, and turkey. Succulent *cochinita* (pork) or *pollo* (chicken) *pibil,* is baked in banana leaves with a sauce of sour orange juice, achiote, and coriander leaves. *Sopa de lima* (lime soup) contains bits of chicken and fried tortillas flavored with lime juice and condiments. Perhaps the favorite, *poc-chuc* is broiled pork flavored with sour oranges and served with marinated and grilled onions, cilantro, and black beans. *Huevos motuleños* constitute a hearty breakfast of fried eggs topped with ham, peas, beans, and cheese, served on a corn tortilla.

The local chile is the *habanero,* perhaps the fieriest in all of Mexico. Luckily for most, the food is usually prepared with small amounts of the pepper, which is then served as a salsa (sauce) alongside the meal. If you like liquers, try the Maya's own Xtabentún, a mixture of fermented honey and anise—best drunk in small sips between bites of fresh lime, which gives a sweet-and-sour effect. The local brews are good but strangely hard to find in peninsular restaurants; these are the dark bock Leon Negra and the light Carta Clara and Montejo. A favorite all over Mexico, Yucatécan *horchata* is made from milled-rice and water, flavored with vanilla. Try the *licuados,* either milk or water based, made with the delicious tropical fruits of the area.

The price classifications of the following restaurants are based on the cost of an average three-course dinner for one person for food alone; beverages and tip would be extra. *Expensive,* $15; *Moderate,* $10–$15; *Inexpensive,* under $10. Abbreviations for credit cards are: AE, American Express; MC, MasterCard; V, Visa. Most restaurants will accept traveler's checks; most *Inexpensive* restaurants do not accept credit cards and do not have phones.

Expensive

Alberto's Continental Patio. Calle 64 #482 at Calle 57; 21 2298. A really charming place for a meal is this mansion from colonial Mexico, full of antiques. Eat indoors or on the garden patio. The menu includes Yucatécan dishes as well as superb Lebanese specialties such as shish kebab and tabouli. For dessert, try the coconut pie, and the Turkish coffee is delicious. AE, MC, V.

Amarantus Paseo Montejo #250 at Calle 1–C; 26 8752. Merida's newest and most popular restaurant has a California decor and serves French-style seafood and meats. MC, V.

Chateau Valentin. Calle 58–A #499–D; 25 5690. A mansion converted into an attractive French restaurant with piano bar. Reservations suggested. AE, MC, V.

Pancho's. Calle 59 #509 between Calles 60 and 62; 23 0942. Restaurant and bar that specializes in flaming drinks of all sorts. Live entertainment some nights on the outdoor patio. AE, MC, V.

Picadilly's. Avenida Pérez Ponce 118; 26 5391. Strictly American fare in an English pub setting. AE, MC, V.

Moderate

Los Almendros. Calle 50A #493, between Calles 57 and 59 on the Plaza de Mejorada; 21 2851. This landmark Mérida restaurant is really a must. During lunch (around 2 P.M.) it's filled with Mexican families and businessmen, not just tourists. The colorful menu describes each dish in Spanish and English, and the food is very good. AE.

La Casona. Calle 60 #434 at Calle 47; 23 8348. Italian restaurant specializing in homemade pasta; situated in a beautiful garden. AE, MC, V.

Le Gourmet, Pérez Ponce 109; 27 1970. Fine dining in a converted mansion. A favorite with the locals. MC, V.

El Portico del Peregrino. Calle 57 #501 between Calles 60 and 62; 21 8468. Both regional and international foods are served in this small garden restaurant, a restored 19th-century home. Tables indoors with air-conditioning or under a canopy of flowering trees. Begin the meal with tortilla soup, or the generous *ceviche* and seafood cocktails. Open daily noon–3 P.M. and 6–11 P.M. AE, MC, V.

Inexpensive

El Guacamayo, Calle 60 Norte at Carretera a Progreso; 25 6690. Regional dishes served in a casual atmosphere. MC, V.

Kon Tiki. Calle 21 #198; 25 4409. Mérida's local Chinese restaurant. MC, V.

Las Mil Tortas. Calle 62 between Calles 65 and 67, across from main bus station. Good tortas (sandwiches on *bolillos,* or rolls) and *licuados.*

La Prosperidad. Corner of Calles 53 and 56; 21 1898. A large noisy restaurant made of palm leaves in the country style. Hor d'ouevres served with your beer. Friendly patrons and people from all parts of Mexico, it seems, welcome the tourist; customers trill their own songs over the microphone. Live music, very loud.

Restaurant Siqueff. Calle 59 #553 between Calles 68 and 70; 24 7465. Cuisine in this large, popular restaurant includes seafood, *churrasco argentino* (Argentine-style beef), and Lebanese dishes.

Soberanis. Paseo Montejo #468 between Calles 39 and 37; 27 7186; and at Calle 60 #483 near Parque Santa Lucía; 23 9872. Inexpensive seafood at this chain restaurant. Little in the way of atmosphere, but good food.

Cafe Pop. Calle 57 between Calles 60 and 62; 21 6844. Frequented by university students from La Universidad de Yucatán, across the street. A good place to have coffee and dessert, or make a meal of *pollo pibil* and lime soup. Friendly atmosphere, air-conditioned.

HOW TO GET AROUND. In Mérida the streets are numbered, not named; most of them are one-way. For those with a sense of direction, this seems the essence of logic; anyone else, it's a bit unnerving. North-south streets have even numbers; the numbers get larger as you go west. East-west streets have odd numbers, and the numbers get larger as you go south. The *zócalo* is an important point of reference: bordered on two sides by Calles 60 and 62, and on opposite sides by Calles 61 and 63. Take the time to study a map, locating the *zócalo* and the streets immediately surrounding it. This will save you a lot of frustration later on, and will accustom you to the hub of the city.

Street addresses are confusing because they don't go according to blocks; for example, the 600s may occupy two or more blocks. Locations are therefore referred to more often by indicating the street on which it is located and the nearest cross street: Calle 64 x 61, or Calle 64 between 61 and 63.

Mérida is a compact city, and most of the places of interest downtown are accessible on foot. Bus service is frequent although somewhat confusing until you master the system. You may want to use a taxi to get to the Paseo Montejo or any extremities of the city. Horse-drawn carriages, called *calesas,* are a pleasant way to see the *zócalo* and the mansions along Paseo Montejo, or to begin an evening's adventure.

By Bus. City buses run from 5 A.M. to midnight every day; they don't run on every street, though, and travel more toward certain destinations or neighborhoods. In the downtown area, buses run east on Calle 59 and west on Calle 61, north on Calle 60 and south along Calle 62. You can catch a bus to Progreso heading north on Calle 56.

By Taxi. Taxis are plentiful in all the main spots of tourist activity: the airport, the *zócalo,* Paseo Montejo, and by Parques Hidalgo and Santa Lucia. Or you can call for one from your hotel or restaurant. The fare should be established in advance because taxis aren't metered, but the average fare is about $2.

By Carriage. *Calesas* are found around the *zócalo* and surrounding street; about $10 is the standard asking price, but if you're into bargaining you may get the price down a bit. The standard tour, which will last between 60 and 90 minutes, is around the *zócalo,* up Paseo Montejo, and back. Or ask to be taken to a specific destination if you have one in mind. If you're lucky, your driver will speak English and be able to point out some places of interest.

By Rental Car. The major international rental agencies have booths at the airport, as well as downtown offices, most of which are on the north side of the *zócalo.* If possible, reserve your car in advance, especially if you want air-conditioning or a larger car. A car is more of a hassle than a help in Mérida itself, but it is a great way to see the ruins and the villages surrounding Mérida.

Rental agencies include the following:

Avis. Calle 57 #507 A (23 6191), Paseo Montejo between Calle 47 and 45 (23 6191), and at the airport (24 7991).

Budget. Prolongación Paseo Montejo #497 (27 8755), at the Holiday Inn, and the airport (24 9791).

Hertz. Calle 55 #479 (23 8975) and at the airport (24 9421).

Thrifty. Next door to the Hotel Colón, Calle 62 #483 (24 1764).

TOURIST INFORMATION. The following are good sources of information once you get to town, but they don't normally send brochures or information through the mail; they just don't have the funds. There are also information kiosks at the airport and under the arcaded front of the Palacio Municipal on the *zócalo.* Pick up a copy of the SECTUR map of Mérida and the state of Yucatán at one of the following locations. It's much more informative than the mimeographed, hand-drawn maps you'll be offered, and it costs only about 25¢.

Chamber of Commerce. Avenida Itzaes #273 at Calle 32 (25 3122 or 25 3033).

Federal Office of Tourism. Calle 61 #470 at Calle 54 (24 9431 or 24 9542).

State Office of Tourism. Calle 86B #499–C (24 9495 or 24 5655).

Tourist Information Center. In the Peon Contreras Theater, Calle 60 at 57, in the ADO bus station, and at the airport.

RECOMMENDED READING. A few sources for pretrip research might be:

Coe, Michael. *The Maya.* New York: Thames Hudson, 1984.

De Landa, Diego. *Yucatan Before & After the Conquest.* Translated from the Spanish by William Gates. Mineola, NY: Dover, 1978.

Stephens, John, L. *Incidents of Travel in Yucatan,* 2 vols. Mineola, NY: University of Oklahoma Press, 1963.

SEASONAL EVENTS. Jan. 6, *El Día de los Reyes Magos* (Day of the Three Wise Men), is the traditional day for giving gifts in Mexico. There are festivals in Tizimin (31 miles north of Valladolid) and Cansahcab (41 miles northeast of Mérida on Hwy. 281).

The week before Lent (**Feb.** or **Mar.,** depending on the year) Mardi Gras, or *Carnaval,* is celebrated in Mérida. There are parades with floats, music and dancing in the streets, and often costume balls. Hotel reservations suggested several months in advance. In Tzucacab, south of Mérida, and Tixkokob, east of Mérida, the holiday is grandly celebrated.

May 3 is the *Day of the Holy Cross,* celebrated in Celestún (on the Gulf of Mexico 55 miles east of Mérida on Hwy. 281); Maxcanu (38 miles southwest of Mérida on Hwy. 180 toward Campeche); and Xocchel (east on Hwy. 180, about 32 miles). There are fireworks and parades, and the ritual Dance of the Pig's Head is celebrated in this blending of Christian and Maya traditions. The final week in May is time to check out the *hammock festival* in Tecoh, about 12 miles south of Mérida. The locals celebrate the beautifully made hammocks, the main source of their livelihood. The final 10 days of May are given over to the *Jipi Festival* in Becal, 51 miles south of Mérida on Hwy. 180. This holiday is in honor of the jipijapa plant, used to make the Panama hats produced in the region.

June 29 is the Day of San Pedro, celebrated in Cacalchen (21 miles east of Mérida on Hwy. 80).

Sometime in early **July** the inhabitants of Ticul celebrate its founding (about 51 miles south of Mérida). The week-long celebration boasts fireworks, handicraft displays, and sports events; there are dances and musical performances.

Mid-July marks the beginning of a 10-day *festival* in which the inhabitants of Dzidzantún honor Santa Clara. An image of the Virgin is carried from Santa Clara, on the gulf coast north of Mérida, to Dzidzantún, 9 miles away, and festivities continue for the next 10 days.

Mid-Sept. is the festival del *Cristo de San Román* in Dzan (53 miles southwest of Mérida on Hwy. 184). There is a religious procession, and pilgrims dance the typical *jaranas*—a Mexican version of the Spanish *jota*. There are bullfights, fireworks, and band music.

Día de San Francisco de Asis is celebrated in Uman, Hocaba, Conkal, and Telchac Pueblo, all near Mérida, on **Oct.** 4. Mérida's two-week festival in honor of *El Señor de las Ampollas* (Christ of the Blisters) culminates on Oct. 13–14 with fireworks, dances, and religious ceremonies.

Oct. 18 is *Día del Cristo de Sitilpech* in Izamal (51 miles east of Mérida). A procession begins the 10-day fiesta. Groups of pilgrims carry offerings of flowers to the church altars; many candles are lit. The *jarana* is danced in the *zócalo.* **Nov.** 1–2, *All Souls' Day* and *All Saints' Day,* known as *Día de los Muertos* (Day of the Dead), when families prepare typical foods to offer departed souls. In Mérida, tables of offerings, favorite foods, incense, flowers, and more are offered to family members in a ritual combining pre-Columbian and Christian traditions.

Nov. 8–13 is *Día de Santiago de Alcalá* in Tekax, 71 miles south of Mérida. Festivities include bullfights and typical dances.

An event important to Méridians is the festival of *Our Lady of Guadalupe* on **Dec.** 12 at the church in her honor. The celebration actually begins on the evening of the 11th, with fireworks, parades, and street carnivals.

On **Dec.** 16–25 the small Yucatécan towns of Espitas and Temax have a particularly interesting way of celebrating *las Posadas, Christmas Eve,* and *Christmas.* The celebration starts with a religious procession simulating the Virgin's search for shelter. During the week, one of Mexico's oldest forms of theater, the *pastorelas,* are performed. Processions and typical dances add flavor to the celebration.

FREE EVENTS. During the week of the *pre-Lenten celebration,* the streets are alive with music and dancing. There are parades, fireworks, and constant merrymaking. Even when there's no festival in Mérida, it seems like almost every evening of the week there is some sort of free music or entertainment. Check the tourist information offices or the *Guía Turística Cultural de Yucatán,* a publication distributed free of charge by the State Tourism Office.

Monday evenings at 9, *regional dances* are performed in the patio of the Municipal Palace on the *zócalo* (or main plaza).

Tuesday evenings at the same time local bands play big-band and other old-time music in Santiago Park.

If you're in Mérida on a Thursday evening, don't miss the *Serenata Yucatéca* performed at 9 P.M. at the Plaza de Santa Lucía, on Calle 60, three blocks north of the main plaza. The program varies, but the traditional *serenata,* music and dance of the region, is presented in some form, often accompanied by a full orchestra. Sometimes *trovas,* or Yucatécan ballads, are performed by a trio of guitarists. The regional *jarana,* a Mexicanized version of the Spanish *jota,* is the standard finale, a pleasant evening for tourists and Mérida residents alike.

Fridays at 9 P.M. the *Serenata Universitaria* is held in the patio of the University. The entertainment in this romantic setting might include guitarists, marimba music, poetry readings, or choral groups. Singers from the audience are sometimes invited to perform.

On Sundays Mérida puts together a program called *Mérida en Domingo.* On the *zócalo,* locals sell jewelry made of beads, shells, and tortoise shell (which can't be brought back into the U.S.), crocheted items, and the like—it resembles a church bazaar more than anything. Sunday cultural events: *Music from the Past* concert, 11 A.M., Parque Santa Lucía; *marimba audition,* noon, Parque Hidalgo; and a *Boda Mestiza* at the *zócalo* at 1 P.M.

TOURS. *Agencia de Viajes González* offers tours to various archaeological sites throughout the peninsula. The tour office is on Calle 59 #476 (28 0228 or 24 8687), Mérida, Yuc., Mexico. Accepts Visa, Mastercard. Price of the tours includes transportation, entrance fee, guide service, and either lunch or dinner. An interesting arrangement is a trip from Mérida to Chichén Itzá, with a drop-off in Cancún after the tour and lunch. Leaves Mérida 9 A.M. daily, arrives in Cancún 7 P.M.; about $35. (The same excursion returning to Mérida at 4:30 P.M. is about $23.) An excursion to Uxmal and Kabah is $15. A tour to the ruins at Sayil, Labná, and Xlapak leaves at 9 A.M., returns at 5 P.M. 2-person minimum, $50 per person.

Ceiba Tours, in the Holiday Inn and at Calle 60 #495 (24 5855), is owned by Roger Piniche, former state director of tourism, who emphasizes quality and employs the best guides available. *La Ceiba* charges more but provides good value.

Mayaland Tours, Avenida Colón #502 between Calles 62 and 60 (25 2133; in U.S. 800–451–8891 or 305–341–9173). Daily tours to Chichén Itzá and/or Uxmal, with overnight accommodations or returning to Mérida same day. The extended tour to Uxmal includes visits to other archaeological sites in the area, and overnight accommodations in the Hotel Hacienda Uxmal. An afternoon visit to Uxmal, including dinner and the light and sound show, costs $39. Tours to Chichén Itzá can be extended with a trip to the Caves of Balancanche, and an overnight stay in the delightful Hotel Mayaland. The excursion to the beach at Progreso stops at the somewhat unimpressive archaeological site of Dzibichaltún. There are also city tours of Mérida every morning and afternoon.

Molica Tours is based in Hotel Caribe, Calle 11 #114, between Calles 26 and 28; 24 8733. (Or write to Depto 10, Itzimna, Merida, Yuc.) It offers a city tour for $8; Chichén Itzá or Uxmal, $22 (includes transportation, guide, meal).

SPECIAL-INTEREST SIGHTSEEING. There are sinkholes, or *cenotes,* in Timul, Chichén, Uxmal, Loltun, Dzibichaltún, San Juan, and other places easily accessible to Mérida. Cenote Dzitnup is a subterranean sinkhole where at midday the light enters from an orifice in the ceiling, creating a strange spectacle. In some places, scuba diving is permitted, for certified divers only; in other cenotes you can swim.

AREAS OF INTEREST AROUND MÉRIDA. The trip to **Progreso** (about 21 miles north of Mérida) or the beaches to the north is a worthwhile venture, and can be combined with a stop at the archaeological ruins at **Dzibilchaltún.** Progreso has been the chief port of entry for the peninsula since 1871, when the port at Sisal proved inadequate for handling large ships transporting henequen. The port is now being expanded to accommodate even larger vessels. But the only reason to visit Progreso is to go to the beach. Many Méridians have summer homes here, and the palm-lined beach is reminiscent of those in Florida. The town, however, is positively deserted on weekdays most of the year—Mérida residents generally vacation in July and August. There are also nice beaches and two new hotels in the town of **Yucalpetén,** about 2 miles west of Progreso, and in **Chicxulub Puerto,** about 2½ miles to the east. In Progreso there are a few restaurants along Calle 19, which runs along the beach, notably Las Velas, Carabela and Capitán Marisco. On the square, Soberanis and Cordobés have reasonably good food at slightly lower prices. Since the bus runs to and from Mérida every 15 minutes 5 A.M.–9 P.M. (leaving Mérida from Calle 62 between 65 and 67), and the trip takes only about 45 minutes, there's no reason to stay in Progreso unless you want to get away from all of humanity. If so, you might try the Hotel Miramar on Calle 30 (also called La Avenida, $12 double room), Hotel Río Blanco ($12 double room), or the *Fiesta Inn* in Yucalpetén, a first-class resort hotel that is part of the *Posadas de México* chain ($50 double room).

Dzibilchaltún (literally, "the place where there is writing on flat stones"), occupying over 25 square miles of land north of Mérida, is thought to have been the capital of the Mayan states at one time. Founded in approximately 2000 B.C., it appears to be the oldest continuously occupied Mayan ceremonial and administrative center. The site is generally more impressive to archaeologists and historians than to tourists, and much of it remains to be explored and excavated. The **Temple of the Seven Dolls** has been restored—the only Mayan temple with windows discovered thus far.

Located on the ruin site is the **Xlacah cenote,** which was apparently a supply of drinking water as well as a ceremonial font. Divers from the National Geographic Society have concluded that victims were sacrificed into the well, based on the number of bones and ceremonial objects found in it. Swimming is permitted on days when research teams are not at work.

A small museum at the entrance to the site displays the seven "dolls" found in the temple, thought to represent different deformities or illnesses, as well as figures and bones from the cenote. There is a small refreshment stand.

Buses to Dzibilchaltún leave 7 times a day from Mérida, at 4:20 A.M., 7:10 A.M., 10:50 A.M., 1:20 P.M., 3:20 P.M., 5:45 P.M., and 7:45 P.M. from the Progreso bus station (Calle 62 between Calles 65 and 67). Those taking the 5:45 or 7:45 buses cannot be assured of a bus returning to Mérida, however. Buses between Mérida and Progreso leave every 15 minutes, but leave you about 2½ miles from the site on Rte. 273.

Thirty-two miles from Progreso on Hwy. 25 is the town of **Sisal,** named for the sisal plant which was shipped from the port in great quantity during the mid-19th century. Today the attractions in Sisal are few, although the town livens up a bit during July and Aug., when Mérida residents come to swim and eat dinner. Hotel Felicidades, located a few minutes' walk up the beach east of the pier, caters to tourists during the vacation months, and can be fun when a crowd arrives, although it is somewhat dingy. Buses bound for Sisal leave regularly from Autotransportes del Sur, Calle 77 #541–C; the trip takes 1½–2 hours.

Celestún is a sleepy little fishing town at the end of a spit of land separating Río Esperanza from the gulf. Popular with Mexican tourists, the beach is pleasant during the day, but it tends to get windy in the afternoon, making the gulf choppy and the sand blow. Bright pink flamingos make the large estuary north of the town their home. The area between Sisal and Celestún is a favorite hunting grounds (see *Sports* section). There are several seafood restaurants on the beach strip, serving mainly seafood. Restaurant Lupita, Calle 10 at Calle 7, can be recommended. Buses leave Mérida for Celestún from Autotransportes del Sur, Calle 77 #541–C. Buses leave every hour or 2 hours; the trip takes around 1½ hours.

PARKS AND GARDENS. Mérida's squares and parks are among her most charming features. There are the small parks; large parks; parks where bands play; parks with zoos and arboritums; parks dedicated to the nation, the saints, and even maternity. The *zócalo,* or main plaza (officially the *Plaza de la Independencia*) is located on the site of the ancient Mayan Temple of H-Chum-caan. It is a charming place to stroll under centuries-old laurel trees and watch Méridians at play. Surrounding the *zócalo* are the government palace, the cathedral, the Casa de Montejo, and the municipal palace, as well as outdoor cafes, banks, and *dulcerias* and *sorbeterias* (candy and ice cream shops).

The square whose official name is *Cepeda Peraza* is known universally as *Parque Hidalgo.* It is located one block northeast of the *zócalo* on Calle 60 and is almost as popular. There are several restaurants on the square, one of which has tables outside, and there are always plenty of people about. One block farther on and you'll come to the tiny plaza popularly called Plaza de la Madre because of the beautiful white statue *Maternidad* (motherhood) located there.

Plaza Santa Lucía, on Calle 60, three blocks north of the *zócalo,* is built on the side of the diminutive church of the same name, erected in 1585. The plaza hosts the Thurs. night *serenatas,* as well as other celebrations during the year. On Day of the Dead, one finds tables here showing typical *ofrendas,* tables artistically arranged with all the departed's favorite things. The park is rather plain, and its main draw are the cultural happenings that frequently take place there.

On a larger scale, *Parque de las Américas* is a great expanse of green, taking up four square blocks surrounding Paseo Colón, with trees from all of the countries on the American continents. It is a nice place for a picnic, and to look at the trees, but it doesn't have a lot in the way of *moviemiento,* as do the squares in town. The public library is here; there's also a children's playground, a band shell, and a large fountain.

El Parque del Centenario (the Park of the Century) is a park stuffed full of amusements, especially for children. Sun. afternoon is the best time to people watch; weekdays you'll have the park more to yourself, especially during the offseason. There is a tiny skyride and a little train. Ponies jog along tree-shaded paths with their small customers. There are boats to row around the green lake, a playground, and a small zoo.

ZOOS. There is a small zoo in the *Parque del Centenario* (mentioned above). It has animals native to the region, as well as a few from other parts. There are some fabulous zoos in other parts of Mexico, but in comparison, this one is somewhat disappointing.

BEACHES. Progreso long has been the port and beach for Mérida, but now nearby Yucalpetén is becoming a playground of note with two attractive hotels recently opened, *Hotel Sian Ka'an* and the *Fiesta Inn.*

CHILDREN'S ACTIVITIES. Children will enjoy the archaeological sites where they can charge around a bit and burn off a bit of energy, although the tours often bore them. When the kids start to look a bit dazed and bleary-eyed, take them to the *Parque del Centenario.* There are enough amusements and animals there to keep them occupied for hours (and enough junk food, as well). There is also a small playground at *Parque de las Américas,* on Paseo Colón. (See *Parks and Gardens* above.) Most children would also enjoy a ride in the horse-drawn *calesas,* which can be found on the streets surrounding the *zócalo.*

PARTICIPANT SPORTS. Hunting is popular in the Yucatán, especially on the northwest coast around Sisal, only 32 miles from Mérida. Nov. through Mar. are the best months for hunting duck and other waterfowl; other prizes include the small jungle deer, quail, and wild boar. Arrangements, especially the importation of firearms, can be complicated. The people at the Holiday Inn branch of *Ceiba Tours,* (25 6389), are experts at cutting through red tape and setting up expeditions, as is *Maya Tours* at Calle 60 #425 (24 2881 or 24 3022). This organization also arranges fishing tours for trips of overnight or longer to Cozumel, Isla Mujeres, Playa del Carmen, and other seaside locations.

    Cave lovers will want to visit the Caves of Loltún, 60 miles southeast of Mérida. Paintings in the illuminated caves are as old as 2,000 years. Guided tours daily at 9:30 and 11 A.M. and 12:30, 2 and 3 P.M., except Mon.

    Golfers will enjoy the 18-hole championship course, at *Club Golf La Ceiba,* 10 miles north of Mérida on the road to Progreso. The course has a club house, bar, and restaurant.

SPECTATOR SPORTS. Bullfights are most often scheduled Dec.–Mar., or to coincide with holidays, though there is no set schedule. Contact the travel desk at your hotel or one of the tourist information centers to see whether any bullfights are scheduled during your stay. **Baseball** is played with enthusiasm in Mexico; the season runs March–July. The stadium is located on Calle 14, #17, right next to the Carta Clara brewery.

HISTORIC SITES AND HOUSES. The *Montejo Family Palace* (Calle 63, on south side of the *zócalo*) was built in 1549 by the powerful Montejo family. Originally covering an entire city block, it was occupied by descendants of the Montejo family until 1970. The part that remains now houses a bank. The large, splendidly restored rooms are filled with antiques. On the facade one can see the Spanish coat-of-arms as well as that of the Montejo family, and two Spanish knights standing on the heads of the vanquished Maya. Open Mon.–Fri., 9 A.M.–1:30 P.M.

    Mérida's cathedral, located on the east side of the *zócalo,* was completed in 1598, after nearly 50 years of labor. It was designed by Juan Miguel de Agüero, who also created Havana's Morro Castle. From the outside, it looks more like a windowless fortress than a cathedral, and within, there is a distinctive lack of the magnificent gold that burnishes other Mexican cathedrals. (The cathedral was ransacked during the Revolution, and it has never been restored.) Look for the Christ of the Blisters *(El Cristo de las Ampollas)*.

LIBRARIES. There is a public library in the Parque de las Américas, on Paseo Colón near Calle 21; and another, *Biblioteca Cepeda Peraza,* on Calle 59 at Calle 58, which includes an extensive archaeology library.

NOTABLE CHURCHES. *La Iglesia de Santa Lucia* is a small church at the edge of the plaza of the same name, 3 blocks north of the *zócalo* on Calle 60. Built in 1575, it became the church assigned to the local black population—slaves and servants of Mérida's wealthy class.

The Church of the Third Order, across from Parque Hidalgo on Calle 60 at 59, was built by the Jesuits in the 17th century. The facade is one of the church's most interesting features, having been constructed with stone blocks taken from the great pyramid at T'Ho, on which traces of Mayan bas relief are still visible (these designs are most evident on the 59th street side of the church).

La Ermita de Santa Isabel, on Calle 63 at 64, is part of a Jesuit hermitage, built in 1743. A resting place for travelers in colonial days, the restored chapel is a pretty place to come at sunset, maybe a good final destination for a ride in a horse-drawn carriage. Next door there's a little garden with a waterfall.

MUSEUMS AND GALLERIES. The *Museum of Archaeology* is housed on the main floor of the lovely Palacio Canton, on Paseo Montejo near Calle 43. This impressive mansion was built for a former governor of Mérida by the architect who designed the Peon Contreras Theater; it later became the governor's official palace. Although many of the better archaeological pieces have been moved to Mexico City, the museum does have some good samples of Mayan handicrafts, mostly jade and sculpture, and some utilitarian objects from daily and ritual life. The top floor of the palace is a gallery where exhibits of modern art are displayed. Purchase postcards, souvenirs, and guidebooks to archaeological sites in the museum store. Museum hours, 8 A.M.–8 P.M.; shop hours, 8 A.M.–2 P.M.; Closed Mon.

Visitors can also look forward to seeing the new anthropology museum, which will be housed in the former penitentiary on Calle 86 #499-C at Calle 59.

The *Museo de Arte Popular* (Folk Art Museum) is located on Calle 59, between Calles 48 and 50. The emphasis here is on Yucatécan art, although handicrafts from all over Mexico are on display. The government-run shop sells samples of these crafts. Open Tues.–Sat., 8 A.M.–8 P.M. Free.

FILMS. Films are the usual assortment; mainly American movies with lots of action, more often than not in English with Spanish subtitles. Since movie-going is a popular diversion, especially with Mexican youths, the cinemas are always crowded, weekdays as well as weekends. *Cine Cantarell,* at Calle 60 #488 (21 3456); *Cinema 59,* Calle 59 between Calles 68 and 70 (no phone); *Cine Fantasio,* Calle 59 at Calle 60 (23 5431).

MUSIC AND DANCE. *Peon Contreras Theater,* on Calle 60 near 57, is a turn-of-the-century opera house. There is usually some sort of performance here any night of the week, including jazz concerts, symphonies, modern dance, ballet, and theatrical performances. The folkloric ballet, *Yucatán y sus Raices,* is usually performed Tues. at 9 P.M. For information (in Spanish) on these and all other performances, call 24 9290 or 24 9389.

The Department of Culture stages music and dance presentations throughout the city. Mon. evenings at 9 you can see regional dances performed in the patio of the Municipal Palace (City Hall), which is on the main plaza. Free.

Local bands play big-band music on Tues. at 9 P.M. at *Santiago Park,* Calles 59 and 72.

Thurs. at *Parque Santa Lucia* (3 blocks north of the *zócalo*) the traditional *serenata* is performed, sometimes accompanied by a full orchestra. *Trovas,* or Yucatécan ballads, are often performed by a trio of guitarists, and the *jarana,* a dance of Yucatécan origin, is the standard evening finale.

Fri. at 9 the *Serenata Universitaria* is held in the patio of the University. The entertainment in this romantic setting might include guitarists, marimba music, poetry readings, or choral groups. Singers from the audience are sometimes invited to perform.

The Sun. menu of cultural events usually includes a morning concert at the *Parque Santa Lucia* and a marimba audition at noon in the *Parque Hidalgo.* Check the hand-lettered sign in front of the Palacio Municipal for the week's events.

SHOPPING. The Yucatán is known for its Panama hats (also called *jipis*); henequen and palm baskets, bags, and mats; leather goods; filigree gold and silver jewelry; *huaraches* (leather sandals) and *guayaberas* (in this steamy climate, the guayabera, a man's shirt with many small pleats, is worn in place of the businessman's suitcoat). Silver, shell, and tortoiseshell jewelry are also available, as are *huipiles* (square embroidered shirts and dresses worn by local women).

The Yucatán is deservedly famous for its colorful hammocks, which are an especially good value here. They are available in cotton, nylon, and silk, as well as the very rough henequen fiber. Cotton is a good choice, and widely available; nylon wears longer and fades less than cotton; silk is the choice of the truly devoted hammock lover. When shopping for hammocks, check the weave to see if it's made with single or double threads laced together (this is easiest to determine up by the loop handles). The double-threaded ones are sturdier and stretch less. Hammocks come in different sizes: *sencillo,* for one person; *doble,* crowded for two and very comfortable for one; *matrimonial,* which is very comfortable for two. Sometimes you'll find gigantic ones called *familiares* (or *matrimoniales especiales*) which can sleep an entire family. Decide what your needs are, and check the strings for quality. Vendors who wander the streets will offer you the cheaply made sencillos first, but may have a few higher quality ones too, should you be knowledgeable enough to ask for them.

If you're truly interested in hammocks, you may want to visit towns where hammock making is the main industry, Tixkokob and Ticul. Inquire politely at houses on the edge of town; some will have hammock frames on the porch in the doorway, and almost everyone in town makes and sells hammocks. In Mérida, check out *El Aguacate,* on Calle 58 #492 at Calle 73 (they will ship your hammocks for you, C.O.D.), or try *El Campesino,* Calle 58 between Calles 69 and 71. Selection is not as large here, but since it's less touristy, the prices may be lower and the salespeople are just as helpful.

You'll definitely want to check out the market *(el mercado)* and see what's available. The market occupies the blocks surrounding the Palacio del Gobierno at Calles 65 and 56. Here you'll find hammocks, huaraches, huipiles, food, flowers, and piñatas, as well as an unbelievable quantity of mundane-looking plastic articles. Bargaining is acceptable all over the market; however, it is an art, and loudly offering a ridiculously low price will not help bring the price down.

There are lots of stores and boutiques on the streets nearby, and also near the *zócalo* on Calles 60 and 59. Here the prices are marked and attempts at bargaining often meet with rather glassy-eyed stares. If you're not of a mind to barter (prices are so cheap here that it's almost painful to), the government-run *Casa de las Artesanías,* on Calle 63 #503 between Calles 64 and 66, sells handicrafts from all over Mexico as well as from the Yucatán. The *Museo Nacional de Arte Popular,* Calle 59 between Calles 48 and 50, also has a good selection and fair prices. On Calle 59 #511 at *Marie-Soleil Boutique* you'll find a nice collection of crafts from around Mexico: Oaxacan black pottery and weavings, ceramic figures, romantic women's clothing, and molas. Open daily 9–9, closed Sun. Down the street, the *Centro Artesanal* is open 9:30 A.M.–2 P.M., 4:30–9 P.M.

For *guayaberas* check out *Guayabera's Jack,* Calle 59 between Calles 60 and 62 and *Genuina Yucateca,* Calle 58 #520.

One of Mérida's nicest boutiques is the *Adán y Eva,* in the Continental Patio Restaurant, at Calles 59 and 64. *Georgia Charukas Couture,* at the entrance to Uxmal features top-quality sportswear and accessories designed by the owner. For French-inspired designs in lightweight cotton fabrics, try *Palacio,* Calle 62 #492 at Calle 71.

For fine filigree gold and silver jewelry, go to *Alfonso Garcia,* Itzaes #587, or *Luis Aquí,* Calle 60 #496. Tortoiseshell objects are on sale at *Curios América,* at Calle 60 #498, and *Curios Mayamex,* at Calle 56 and Calle 57.

For books about regional themes, from cooking to archaeology, try the small *Libreria Dante* on Parque Hidalgo. For film and photographic supplies go to *Foto Servicios Omega,* corner of Calle 60 and 59, or *Foto Plaza,* Calle 63 #896.

NIGHTLIFE AND BARS. Mérida has a variety of bars and discos, although for many the evening entertainment centers around dining and watching a performance of regional music and dance. An inexpensive and less touristy alternative is to take in one of the events presented many nights in the city's plazas. These range from entirely professional to something close to amateur hour; but they are always entertaining, and offer an opportunity to see the Mérida residents without their plumed costumes (see *Free Events,* above).

Folkloric ballet is presented nightly (except Fri. and Sun.) at 8 in the *Hotel Calinda Panamericana,* Calle 59 between Calles 52 and 54. Watch the pageantry from the restaurant or from the piano bar. After the dinner show, the nightclub offers "alive" music and shows at 11:30 P.M. and again at 1:30 A.M.

There's live music at *Amarantus Video Bar,* Paseo Montejo # 250 at Calle 1–C (26 8752).

Los Tulipanes, on Calle 42 #462-A (27 2009). Dancers perform nightly, beginning at 8:30, with a Mayan-inspired show in this nightclub –restaurant–disco. Appeals to those with an expansive sense of theater. The food is mediocre, but people enjoy it anyway.

The *Holiday Inn* and *Montejo Palace* both have good live entertainment at night. Top discos are *Excess,* the *Bim Bon Bao, Oasis,* and *Cocoon* at the *Calinda Panamericana.*

COZUMEL

Oft-Discovered Treasure Trove

by
JANE ONSTOTT

Cozumel is a wonderful place to discover, and it seems that this Caribbean treasure chest is constantly being reopened. The original island hoppers were the Mayas themselves; pilgrims from the mainland regularly made the sea trip to Cozumel, location of the only known Mayan oracle. Women flocked to the island to seek the blessings of fertility and protection during childbirth from Ixchel, goddess of childbearing and the moon, among other things.

Cortés found the Mayan religious center in 1518, and stayed long enough to desecrate the temple before reconnoitering with the rest of the Spanish fleet and sailing to Veracruz, where the conquest of Mexico began in earnest. Henry Morgan, the English buccaneer, and other undesirables recognized Cozumel's potential, conveniently located near the crossroads of the Indies spice trade route, and used the island as a base from which to pursue their pirating adventures.

Cozumel was again rediscovered during World War II, this time by the military. American special diving teams came to the island to train before embarking for Europe and the Pacific. These divers, despite the gravity of their mission, left the island with tales of the incredible reefs hugging the island's southern shore, and the crystalline quality of the turquoise water. When Jacques Cousteau declared the Palancar and surrounding reefs to be among the best in the world, the whole world got in on the discovery, and the island of Cozumel is now visited by travelers from around the world, seeking to be blessed by the modern goddess of sun, fun, and scuba.

Diving Is Main Attraction

Scuba diving is still very much what Cozumel is all about. The island has the ambience of a tropical ski town, combining aquatic athletics and evening lollygagging. Young people congregate at the many open-sided cafes to plan dive trips as they drink beer and margaritas. The world-famous Palancar reef is only one of the 20 or so charted reefs in the area praised for their complex coral formations, variety of sealife, and marvelous visibility—100 feet or more made possible by the benevolent Gulf Stream.

Although diving aficionados had the place to themselves for a few years, Cozumel (which comes from a Mayan word meaning "Land of the Swallows") is now visited by cruise ships almost daily. Tourism is the main industry here, yet 90 percent of the island is still untouched and the beaches are still relatively uncrowded. The government, seeking to protect Cozumel's main tourist draw, has declared the 20-mile stretch of reefs to be a national underwater reserve. This is to maintain as much as possible the pristine condition of the beaches while adding the convenience of dive shops, restaurants, and other amenities. Basically, however, the island is little changed.

When the Spanish first visited Cozumel, they estimated it had a population of 40,000; today the population is about half that. The only town, San Miguel de Cozumel (called by most simply "el pueblo") is a fishing community grown big. Duty-free shops line the Malecón—the main drag along the waterfront; prices are marked in dollars and the salespeople greet you in English. The shell jewelry, and coral trinkets are not exactly bargains, but with the strong dollar-peso relationship, you can still bring back relatively inexpensive mementos of your trip.

There are resort hotels located both to the north and south of town. The southern resorts cater to divers, although many of the young divers stay at the less expensive lodgings in town. The northern beach resorts attract many fishermen; the islanders are fond of saying that while first-timers go to Cancún, the real pros come to Cozumel. Billfish usually bite only during the spring; tuna and barracuda are the gamefish the rest of the year. Hotels on both cardinal compass points have excellent facilities for sunbathing, and equipment for snorkeling. Windsurfing and other water sports are widely available.

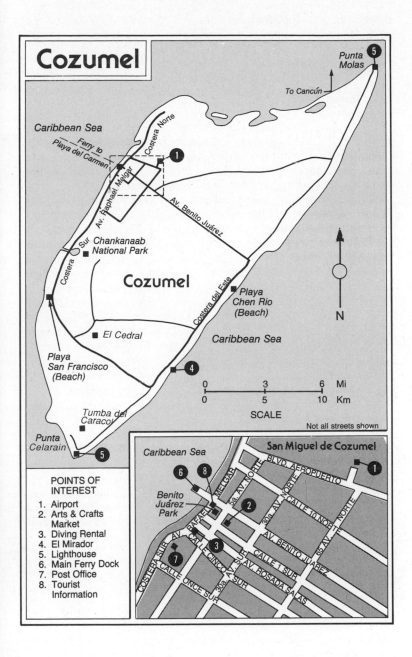

Cozumel

Caribbean Sea

To Cancún →

Punta
Molas

5

Costera Norte

Ferry to
Playa del Carmen

1

Av. Raphael Melgar

Av. Benito Juárez

Costera Sur

Chankanaab
National Park

Cozumel

Costera del Este

Playa
Chen Rio
(Beach)

Caribbean Sea

N

El Cedral

Playa
San Francisco
(Beach)

4

Tumba del
Caracol

0   3   6 Mi
0   5   10 Km
SCALE

Not all streets shown

Punta
Celarain

5

POINTS OF INTEREST

1. Airport
2. Arts & Crafts Market
3. Diving Rental
4. El Mirador
5. Lighthouse
6. Main Ferry Dock
7. Post Office
8. Tourist Information

Caribbean Sea

San Miguel de Cozumel

1

BLVD. AEROPUERTO

6   8

5a. AV. NORTE

10a. AV. NORTE

CALLE 10 NORTE

Benito
Juárez
Park

AV. MELGAR

2

3a. AV. NORTE

5a. AV. NORTE

AV. BENITO JUÁREZ

AV. RAFAEL

CALLE 5a. SUR

3

CALLE 1 SUR

AV. ROSADA SALAS

COSTERA SUR AV.

7

CALLE CINCO AV. SUR

3a. AV. SUR

CALLE ONCE SUR

Cruises and Excursions

Most people set aside a day for what are called Robinson Crusoe cruises—picnic excursions down the coast to some stretch of isolated beach. As the area is now a sea-life sanctuary, the crew no longer dives for fresh conch and lobster en route. The provisions they bring along, however, they grill for an incredible seafood picnic.

Many tourists enjoy a day at the Maya ruins at Tulum, accessible by small plane, boat, ferry, or bus. Others enjoy an overnight stay at the site of the Mayan ruins in Chichén Itzá, in the dense peninsular jungle. Cozumel's own ruins do not compare to these impressive examples of ancient architecture, and their inaccessibility makes them hardly worth the effort it takes to get to them.

Sightseeing on Cozumel itself is pretty limited. The main road loops around to the solitary windward side, where there is one small inn and a couple of small restaurants. The beaches here are beautiful and largely deserted, although the sand is not quite as fine and white as on the lee shore. Swimming on this side is considered dangerous, although there are a few coves and marked beaches along the southern shore around the *Mirador,* or lookout point.

The atmosphere in Cozumel is easy-going; people wear their shorts and T-shirts to restaurants and don't worry a lot about what people will think—no high heels or neckties here. Whether staying in town or at one of the resorts, the daytime focus is on the incredibly light and transparent blue and green waters of the Caribbean; at night the gaze is sleepily shifted to dinner and drinks before diving, exhausted, into one's bed.

PRACTICAL INFORMATION FOR COZUMEL

HOW TO GET THERE. Cozumel is accessible by plane, ferry, and hydroplane. Major airlines fly into Cozumel each day, and there are nonstop flights from cities such as Miami, Houston, Veracruz, and Villahermosa. Puddlejumpers from both Playa del Carmen and Puerto Morelos make the round-trip to the island about seven times a day. Ferries make the round-trip to Cozumel daily from both Playa del Carmen and Puerto Morelos, but the schedules change frequently, and occasionally the ferry doesn't leave port at all, despite the schedule. The catamaran water jet is a modern speed vessel that takes about 30 minutes to bridge the 12-mile gap between Playa del Carmen and Cozumel, as compared to an hour for the ferry.

By Air. *Mexicana* has offices on Avenida Melgar Sur # 17 (2 0157 or 2 0263). *American, Continental,* and *United* airlines fly to Cozumel from major cities in the United States. Flights from Cancún and Playa del Carmen are available via *Aerocozumel* (2 0877). From Playa del Carmen, the current fare is $8, and takes only 7 minutes. Flights leave about every 2 hours, beginning at around 7:30 A.M.—the same for return flights. From

Cancún, the 20-minute trip costs under $30; it also leaves every 2 hours, beginning at 8:30 A.M. U.S. travel agents have minimal information about these small airlines, and flights may have to be arranged on the Yucatán Peninsula. If you can't book the flight as part of your air package, check with a travel agent upon arrival in Mexico.

By Sea. The **ferry** from Puerto Morelos accommodates both people and vehicles. It is inexpensive, currently about $8.50 for automobiles; $16 for RVs; and under $1 per person. The schedule changes frequently, and ferries are often behind schedule. It is fairly safe to assume that the ferry makes one or two round-trips every day except Monday. It leaves Cozumel from the international pier in front of the Hotel Sol Caribe to the south of town. The trip takes about 3 hours and should not be undertaken on an empty stomach. Tickets are on sale approximately 2 hours before departure.

The ferry from Playa del Carmen costs about $1. It leaves from the dock at Playa del Carmen (on the beach just south of the plaza—you can't miss it) approximately every 2 hours between 4 A.M. and 6 P.M. The journey takes from 40 minutes to 1 hour. (Verify the schedule—it changes frequently!)

Waterjet trimarans connect Cozumel (downtown pier) with Playa del Carmen and cost $2. The trip to and from Playa del Carmen takes just 20 minutes, and leaves twice a day. Tickets go on sale at the main pier one hour before departure. To confirm schedule, call 2 1508 or 2 1588.

TELEPHONES. The area code for the island is 987. Long-distance calls can be placed from 2 storefront locations: Avenida 5 and Calle 2 Norte; or on Calle 1 Sur (on the plaza); between the hours of 8 A.M.–1 P.M. and 4–9 P.M. Even easier is to call from your hotel; this service is usually available, especially at the resort hotels. Note that it is much cheaper to call collect; dialing direct is heavily-taxed, and about 60% more expensive than calling collect.

ACCOMMODATIONS. The activity on Cozumel centers around San Miguel de Cozumel, the only town on the island. Budget hotels are for the most part located in town, and the resorts are located to the north and south. These resorts are on some of Cozumel's most beautiful beaches—particularly San Juan and Santa Pilar beaches, on the northern hotel strip. Most of the resort hotels provide water-sports equipment and arrange excursions. Scuba divers and snorkelers usually frequent the hotels on the beaches to the south, where reefs abound; those interested in sailing and fishing generally favor the resorts to the north.

All hotels listed as *Expensive* below have air-conditioning and restaurants. Most *Expensive* and *Moderate* hotels accept credit cards; *Inexpensive* hotels often accept only cash or traveler's checks. Based on double-occupancy rooms during high season (Dec. 15–Apr.), prices are as follows: *Deluxe,* $125–$200 *Expensive,* $85–$125; *Moderate,* $50–$85; *Inexpensive,* under $50.

Deluxe

Hotel Fiesta Americana Sol Caribe. 4 miles south of town; 2 0700; in U.S., 800–223–2332. A geometrically shaped hotel with 220 modern rooms and suites, some more rundown than others. Full range of water-sports activities, tennis courts, free-form pool. Garden bar, 2 restaurants—1 by the pool, 1 for dinner.

Stouffer Presidente. About 6 miles south of town; 2 0322 or 2 0278; in U.S., 800–472–2427. Managed by the country's largest chain, this 259-room resort is one of the best on the island. Excellent snorkeling from the beach. Outstanding restaurant. Full service; tennis, pool.

Expensive

Cabanas del Caribe. North of town, at San Juan beach; 2 0017. Pleasant cottages are sprinkled among flowering trees and coconut palms. Relaxed atmosphere for diving, snorkeling, Windsurfing. Restaurant and bar by the beach; tennis, pool.

Club Cozumel Caribe. North of town at San Juan beach; 2 0100. An all-inclusive resort with one price covering meals and activities. There's usually a minimum 3-night stay.

Galapago Inn. South of town; 2 0663. A pretty, white stucco hotel popular with divers. Tiled benches surround a small fountain in the central garden. Rates include meals and 2 days of diving; 3-night minimum stay required.

Hotel El Cozumeleno. North of town, at Santa Pilar beach; 2 0344, Box 53, Cozumel, Quintana Roo, Mexico. Restaurant, pool, tennis, Ping-Pong, volleyball. Fishing expeditions, car rentals. Outside bar serves tables under thatched umbrellas.

Hotel La Ceiba. South of town; 2 0379; in U.S., 800–221–6509; on East Coast, 800–221–9580. Popular with divers, this attractive high-rise hotel has large, comfortable rooms. Tennis, large swimming pool, swim-up hot tub bar; sauna and gym. Sunken DC–3 off the coast provides a hideout for fish and a haven for divers.

Hotel La Perla. 2 miles south of town; 2 0188. This cozy hotel with just 22 rooms and 1 suite is a quiet, comfortable haven. Small beach with pier and launch. Swimming pool, sundeck.

Melía Mayan Cozumel. Northernmost hotel on Cozumel, at Santa Pilar beach; 2 0411. Modern 14-story hotel. Windsurfing and other water-sports equipment available; glass-bottom boat tours. Snack bar at the water's edge under Tahiti-styled thatched roofs. 2 swimming pools, 1 with swim-up bar. Tennis courts, gift shop, rental cars.

Moderate

Hotel Bahia. Avenida Rafael Melgar #25 at Calle 3 Sur, 2 0209. Kitchenettes, telephone and TV in rooms, air-conditioning.

Hotel Cantarell. North of town, at San Juan beach; 2 0144. One of Cozumel's oldest hotels, with comfortable rooms. Located on a long, thin stretch of beach, with a pool and a Jacuzzi. Restaurant, bar; snack stand on the beach.

Hotel Mara. Just north of town, at San Juan Beach; 2 0300. One of the best in its price range. 50 good-sized rooms, all with ocean view and either balcony or access to sundeck. Dive shop, scuba and snorkel equipment, instruction, and tours; glass-bottom boats; children's and adults' pools; beach access. Dinner music in the evening.

Hotel Playa Azul. North of town, at San Juan beach; 2 0199. 27 bungalows and 30 suites—a bit more pleasant by the beach than in the suite. Pool. Popular with families.

Meson San Miguel. Avenida Juarez #2, north side of plaza; 2 0233. One of the largest of the downtown hotels, with 97 carpeted rooms, bar, air-conditioning, swimming pool, and telephones.

Villa Blanca. South of town; 2 0730. 50 nice rooms with sunken bath-tubs; nicely landscaped grounds. Dive shop, restaurant, and dock across the street. Pool and tennis courts.

Inexpensive

Bungalows Pepita. 2 blocks east of the plaza, at Avenida 15 Sur, 2 0098. A pleasant economy hotel with 30 rooms in two buildings. Rooms are clean and some have refrigerators. Newer rooms have air-conditioning and ceiling fans; older rooms have ceiling fans only.

Hotel Mary Carmen. 1 block south of the plaza at Avenida 5 Sur #4; 2 0581. Carpeted rooms open onto attractive garden courtyard. Air-conditioning. No restaurant.

Hotel Paraiso Caribe. Avenida 5 Norte #599, on the road to the air-port; 2 0740. The 37 rooms have no air-conditioning but do have ceiling fans. Pool, garden, coffee shop, and bar.

Hotel Suites Bazar Colonial. One block south of main plaza at Avenida 5 Sur #9; 2–05–06. This attractive 3-story hotel "bazar" has it all: travel agency, Banamex office, car rentals, and boutiques. Suites have fully equipped kitchenettes with refrigerators; some rooms have balconies.

Hotel Suites Elizabeth. Calle Adolfo Salas #3, 1 block south of the plaza; 2 0330. Comfortable, air-conditioned rooms and suites with kitch-enettes face onto an attractive central garden. Some rooms have balconies; air-conditioning.

Hotel Vista del Mar. Avenida Rafael Melgar #45; 2 0545. Some of the 26 rooms have balconies and an ocean view. Nice coffee shop and pool. Dive shop, car rentals.

DINING OUT. Dining out in Cozumel is a casual affair. Many water-sports enthusiasts get up early to ply their sports all day, and are ready for a hearty evening meal by 7, which is early by Mexican standards, but perfectly acceptable on Cozumel. The resort hotels on the north and south beaches have their own restaurants, but it's often more fun to search out new dining experiences than to eat in the familiar surroundings of the hotel. The following restaurants are categorized as follows, based on the cost of a 3-course meal for one, and not including beverages, tax, or tip: *Expensive,* $20 and up *Moderate,* $10–$20; *Inexpensive,* under $10. Abbre-viations for credit cards are: AE, American Express; CB, Carte Blanche; D, Diners Club; MC, MasterCard; V, Visa. Most restaurants will accept traveler's checks.

Expensive

Café del Puerto. On the main plaza; 2 0316. Seafood grill, lobster, and prime rib are the specialties. The setting is romantic with a guitar and piano playing softly in the background. Open from 5 P.M. to midnight. AE, MC, V.

Carlos 'n Charlie's and Jimmy Kitchen. On the Malecón, 1½ blocks north of the main plaza; 2 0191. A nice view of the stars and the Malecón, and a busy, holiday atmosphere, make this a popular restaurant-bar. Spe-cialties include excellent beef ribs and seafood; there is a good selection of other dishes as well. Open from 10 A.M. to midnight; Sun. from 5 P.M. to midnight. MC, V.

Las Palmeras. Between the main plaza and the Malecón; 2 0532. Near the ferry dock, a good place to cool one's heels and snack as well as dine. This indoor-outdoor restaurant is popular with both locals and tourists.

Morgan's. On the plaza; 2 0584. Full of polished wood, and looks like it belongs on the coast of New England. Open for both lunch and dinner, with tropical music in the evenings. The place to go for a big night out. Reservations suggested. AE, D, MC, V.

Plaza Leza. On the main plaza; 2 1041. A sidewalk cafe with an indoor garden restaurant. Open from 7 A.M. until midnight. AE, MC, V.

Pepe's Grill. On the Malecón 1 block south of the main plaza; 2 0213. Popular with tourists and known for its seafood and steaks. AE, DC, MC, V.

The Sports Page. Corner of Avenida 5 and Calle 2; 2 1199. The hangout for Americans who don't want to miss Monday Night Football (beamed in via satellite) and enjoy familiar foods, including fried chicken, steaks, and seafood. Open for breakfast as well as lunch and dinner. MC, V.

Moderate

La Laguna. In Chankanaab National Park. A good place to eat lunch after sunning and snorkeling. It's open 10 A.M.–4 P.M. only, and seafood is naturally the specialty. On the beach, tables are covered by thatched roofs. MC, V.

Pizza Rolandi. 3½ blocks north of main plaza on Avenida Rafael Melgar. The pretty outdoor garden is the perfect place to enjoy Rolandi's refreshingly different Italian recipes, including pizza with shrimp, asparagus, or fresh tomato, as well as delicious antipasto and other expertly seasoned items. Try some amaretto or coconut ice cream for dessert. Good music at just the right volume. Open 12–12. AE, CB, D, MC, V.

El Portal. On the waterfront just across from the main ferry; 2 0316. Serves breakfast. This casual cafe, full of photos of old Cozumel, is a good spot to try Yucatécan specialties. MC, V.

Inexpensive

El Foco. 5 Avenida Sur, 1½ blocks south of main plaza. A small but lively place where graffiti-writing on the walls is encouraged. Casual atmosphere, good food.

Las Tortugas. Avenida 10 Norte #82, 2½ blocks northeast of main plaza. Serves beer and a variety of tacos, tortas, and other spicy staples. Popular with rowdy dive groups.

HOW TO GET AROUND. One main road traverses the island of Cozumel, connecting the north end to the southern tip, circling up past several small ruin sites, and heading back north along the windward side of the island. Halfway along this stretch of beach, the road returns to the more populous leeward side. Most of the traffic, both pedestrian and vehicular, is concentrated in town. Avenida Rafael Melgar, often referred to as *el Malecón* where it parallels the waterfront in the central district, is the main drag. The main pier is located on the Malecón just west of the plaza. Cruise ships dock at the international pier south of town in front of the Hotel Sol Caribe.

Bus service is poor (surprising in Mexico, but in Cozumel everyone seems to have a scooter). VW vans provide transportation in from the airport for a couple of dollars, up to $5 for one passenger.

Taxis are relatively inexpensive, about $2–$3 between town and the hotels north or south of town. Especially when shared by two or more, taxis probably represent the best bargain for those who plan to make a couple of excursions each day to town or to the beach. Taxis can easily be found on the Malecón, or around the plaza, especially on the southeast corner. The taxi office is on 2 Calle Norte, one block north of the plaza and half a block from the waterfront (2 0236 and 2 0041).

Rental cars and **motor scooters** are available for those who want more mobility. Cars start at about $50 a day; motorbikes are about $20. While motorbikes are very popular on the island, they can be dangerous in town, and insurance for them is nonexistent. The only gas station in town is located at Avenida Juarez and 30 Avenida Sur, about 5 blocks east of the main plaza. It is allegedly open 7 days a week, between 7 A.M. and 11 P.M.

Rentals agencies include the following:

Avis. At Hotel Presidente (2 0322); at Calle 20 between Rodolfo Salas and Calle 3 Sur (2 1923), and at the airport (no phone). Cars only.

Budget. Avenida 5 #9 (2 0903) between Calle 2 Norte and Calle 4 Norte; and at the airport (no phone). Cars and jeeps.

Fiesta Cozumel. Avenida Sur #11 (2 0725). Cars and mopeds.

Rentadora Caribe. Calle Rosado Salas #3 (2 0955). Motorbikes only.

Rentadora Cozumel. Calle Rosado Salas #3–B (2 1429); and Avenida 10 between Rosado Salas and 1st Sur (2 1120). Bicycles and motorbikes.

TOURIST INFORMATION. Cozumel's tourist office is located on the second floor of the Plaza del Sol building on Avenida Juárez and Avenida 5 Sur (2 0972), facing the main plaza. There are information booths on the plaza and at the pier. The information available at these offices is mainly in the form of 2 free booklets, combinations of paid advertising and tourist information, which you can get just as easily at most hotels, as well as shops and restaurants. These booklets are useful, and the English translations will provide you with hours of amusement: *Cozumel, What to Do, Where to Go;* and *The Blue Guide to Cozumel.* The "brown map" is the best map available of the island, and is sold in local shops and at the airport.

Exchange money at *Bancomer* or *Banco Atlántico,* both located around the main plaza, between the hours of 9:30 A.M. and 12:30 P.M. The main post office is located on Avenida Melgar at Calle 7 Sur, on the south side of town; telegraph office is located in the same building. Hours are Mon.–Fri., 9 A.M.–1 P.M. and 3–6 P.M.; Sat. 9 A.M.–3 P.M. The Red Cross is located at Avenida Rosado Salas at 20 Avenida Sur (2 1058).

SEASONAL EVENTS. *Carnaval,* or Mardi Gras, is celebrated with fervor on the island of Cozumel. The date of this pre-Lenten festival varies each year, but usually falls sometime in **February.** There are usually costume balls, and often fireworks and parades. *Santa Cruz Fiesta* is celebrated **May** 3 in El Cedral to mark the discovery of Cozumel by Europeans. **June** 1 marks Navy Day. **June** 28–29 is the *Feast of St. Peter and St. Paul,* when the dance of the Pig's Head takes place. **September** 29, the *Day of San Miguel,* patron saint of the island, is marked with the biggest fiesta of all with a procession of decorated boats as well as parades and dancing. In **May** and **June** billfish tournaments are held, bringing to Cozumel fishermen from all over the continent.

TOURS. Even though Cozumel is Mexico's largest island, anyone staying for a week or so may begin to get island fever. The antidote is a tour of the fabulous archaeological sites at Chichén Itzá or Tulum. The tours listed below can be arranged through *Fiesta Cozumel*, which has agents at most of the large hotels. Or call the main office at 2 0522 or 2 0433. Fiesta Cozumel also offers an island tour combining shopping at a black coral factory with a visit to the beach on the windward side of the island, ending at Chankanaab Lagoon for snorkeling and sunbathing. The tour lasts approximately 6 hours. *Viajes y Deportes del Caribe,* in the lobby of the Hotel Stouffer Presidente (2 0923 or 2 0322) offers many of the same tours, as well as horseback tours into the jungle, island tours highlighting the ruins at San Gervasio, glass-bottom boat tours, and sailing tours.

A 40-minute **plane ride** brings the ruins of Chichén Itzá comfortably close. The site itself is beautiful, the main pyramid impressive, and the plane ride provides a great aerial view of the thick jungle. Definitely a worthwhile excursion.

Another interesting day trip is a tour of Tulum, the only major site occupied at the time of the Spaniard's arrival. After the short flight to Playa del Carmen, a 2-hour bus ride brings you to the ruins at Tulum. After the guided tour of the ruins, you'll stop at the natural lagoon of Xel-Ha, a snorkeling paradise, where equipment can be rented. After an hour or so of snorkeling, swimming, or sunning, tours regularly stop for lunch at the beach resort of Akumal, returning to Cozumel in the late afternoon.

Robinson Crusoe **boat tours** will deposit you in the morning on a pretty beach on the southern shore. Lunch is later prepared, island style: usually fish or conch grilled on an open fire. The boat stops for snorkeling at a shallow coral reef on the way back, about 4 P.M. Equipment can be rented, although it is not included in the price.

Deep-sea fishing can be arranged on **charter boats,** which leave the downtown pier at 9 A.M. and return at 4 P.M. Prices depend on the season and number of people (up to 4) but should run $300–$500 for a boat for 4 fishermen.

Fiesta Cozumel also offers snorkel and **dive trips,** as do the numerous dive shops on the island. Most of the resort hotels have dive shops on the premises or are connected with one downtown. The following establishments offer a variety of dive trips as well as equipment rentals. Most offer day trips, half-day trips, and night dives as well as certification training and refresher courses. The price for a full-day boat dive ranges from $40 to $50. Night dives usually have a 3-person minimum and cost about $20. Price usually covers the cost of the boat, guide, and lunch; equipment rental is extra. Snorkelers can often accompany divers on the same trip for about $30.

Aqua Safari Dive Shop, on the waterfront at Calle 5 South (2 0101 or 2 0661).

Caribbean Divers, Avenida Melgar #38B, P.O. Box 191, Cozumel, Q.R. (2 1080 or 2 1426). Accepts credit cards.

Dive Paradise, Avenida Rafael Melgar 601, Cozumel, Q.R., Mexico, 77600 (2 1007 or, in the U.S., 800–247–3483 or 206–441–3483).

Viajes y Deportes del Caribe, Hotel Stouffer Presidente (2 0923 or 2 0322). Snorkel also.

SPECIAL-INTEREST SIGHTSEEING. If you're into **bird-watching,** bring your binoculars, especially if your island vacation is in spring or fall, when North American migrants fill the woodlands of the interior, and feast on seeds in the fields. As in most climes, the best time to bird-watch is at dawn, when the birds are feeding; they quiet down considerably by

9 in the morning. Among the birds you'll see are the frigate, Yucatán woodpecker, tropical pewee, Caribbean elaenia, black catbird, the stripe-headed tanager, the rose-throated tanager, and others.

Glass-bottom boats are a thrilling way to explore coral formations, teeming with sea life, without even getting your feet wet. Tours available through *Viajes y Deportes del Caribe* (see *Tours* Section above) as well as many beachfront hotels.

The ruins on the island are insignificant when compared to those on the mainland, but if you're not planning to leave the island you may want to visit **El Cedral,** once the island's population center (turn left onto the dirt road just past San Francisco Beach). The temple is small and dilapi-dated, but somewhat interesting. Next to the temple is a small, modern church in which rows of small crosses are draped with intricately embroi-dered mantles, following a tradition that probably dates to the War of the Castes.

To get to the **Tumba del Caracol,** a small ruins site where the Mayas once worshipped, take the road to the windward side of the island, and go down the dirt road toward the lighthouse at Punta Celarain. Continue on down this dirt road to view the lighthouse, then drive a few more miles to find a nice secluded beach, at the island's southernmost tip. The ruins at San Gervasio, one of 34 small sites on the island, have not been excavat-ed, and it's really not worth the effort to bump down the dirt trail that leads to them.

PARKS AND GARDENS. *Chankanaab,* which in Maya means "small sea," is a beautiful national park, both above and below the water. The natural aquarium has been designated as an underwater preserve for the more than 50 species of tropical fish that make it their home, as well as crustaceans and coral. Snorkeling and scuba equipment can be rented, and instruction and professional guides are available, as are courses for diving certification.

Almost as interesting as the underwater life are the over 300 species of tropical plants, both imported and indigenous, found around the la-goon. La Laguna restaurant serves food and beverages 9 A.M.–4 P.M.; gift shops are open 9:30 A.M.–4 P.M.

BEACHES. Beaches are what Cozumel is all about. The best of the white sand beaches are on the leeshore (west side of the island), especially *Santa Pilar* and *San Juan* beaches, which run along the northern hotel strip. You won't be alone here, but you will be able to order a soft drink, or rent water-sports equipment if you're in the mood. (All beaches on Co-zumel are public access, so you don't have to be staying at a hotel to use the beach in front of it.) The southwestern shore boasts the longest beach, about 2½ miles long. There are some restaurants and water sports facili-ties here at *Playa Maya,* as well as at *Playa San Francisco,* a popular beach (admission is about a quarter, open 8 A.M.–5 P.M.). Food and equipment rental is a bit more expensive here than on the more frequented beaches.

Punta Celarain is a beautiful, secluded beach located at the southeast tip of the island. To get there turn right onto the dirt road when you reach the windward side of the island (go toward the lighthouse). Or continue on the main road, turning left when you reach the windward side. There is a lookout point called El Mirador, where one gets a good view of the waves crashing against the rocks, and secluded beaches nestled in coves at Punta Chiquero (stop in for ceviche at The Naked Turtle restaurant) and Chen Río. The ocean on this side of the island is rougher, and swimming is considered more dangerous here because of the strong undertow.

SPORTS. Scuba diving is undoubtedly the most popular sport on the island, with snorkeling a close second. (See *Tours* section for rental information.) Palancar, the most famous of Cozumel's reefs, is actually a conglomeration of different coral formations stretching for almost 3 miles, and is only one of some 20-odd reefs charted for diving off the southwest coast. Excellent offshore dropoffs and fringing reefs are home to small snapper, sergeant majors, parrot fish, butterflyfish, and grouper. The reefs stretch for 20 miles beginning at the international pier and continuing on to Punta Celarain on the southernmost tip of the island. The Gulf Stream makes visibility of 100 feet routine, and at Palancar and Colombia Reefs, 250-foot visibility is not uncommon. Beginning divers will find low-profile reefs brilliant with star coral, giant brain coral, and fire coral, as well as sponges of strange and beautiful shapes, angelfish, and other reef tropicals. Experienced divers will find opportunities to test their diving skills at challenging reefs such as Maracaibo, a deep reef laced with tunnels, caves, and crevices.

Snorkelers frequent many of the same reefs as the scuba divers, including the beaches in front of the Hotel La Ceiba, where a sunken DC-3 attracts an army of fish, Chankanaab Heads, lying about 20 yards off the beach at Chankanaab, and Colombia Lagoon.

Deep-sea fishing is a year-round adventure on Cozumel, but the prime season for marlin and sailfish is March and mid-July, and barracuda, red snapper, bonito, kingfish, and tarpon are also in abundance. Billfish are especially sought after during the months of May and June, when both Cancún and Cozumel host tournaments. Excursions to the lagoon in the northern part of the island, south of Tulum on the mainland, are popular, especially for bonefishing. Boats can be chartered through the resort hotels on the northern beaches, notably *Cabanas del Caribe* and *Melía Mayan Cozumel,* as well as through the boatman's syndicate on the main pier (2 0080); the *Club Naútico de Cozumel,* about a mile north of town on the Carretera Costera Norte (2 1113); and *Aquarius Travel,* Avenida 3 Sur #2 (2 1092), which specializes in bonefishing. Small boats can be hired at the pier for a day's fishing.

Windsurfers can be rented on the beach in front of the *Hotel Melía Mayan Cozumel* north of town, and at the *Hotel Sol Caribe* and the *El Presidente* on the south side, and at many of the smaller hotels.

Bicycles and **motorbikes** are available from several rental agencies. *Rentadora Cozumel* (2 1120) will deliver bikes to your hotel.

FILMS. There are two cinemas on Cozumel. *Cinema Cozumel* is located at Avenida Melgar at Calle 4. *Cine Cecilio Borges* is on Avenida Juarez at Avenida 35. Both theaters list show times at 9:15 P.M., but since long lines can be seen in front of them at various times of day, it is advisable to check show times at the theater to be sure. Movies are often in English with Spanish subtitles.

MUSIC AND DANCE. Las Gaviotas, a restaurant–bar within Cabañas del Caribe Hotel, has a Thurs. dinner show featuring Mexican singing and dancing, beginning at 7:30 P.M. Sun. dinner show features mariachis and begins at 6:30 P.M. Call 2 0877 for reservations.

SHOPPING. A "bargain" is a relative term. While prices in Cozumel are higher than those in many less-frequented parts of Mexico, the deflation of the peso makes handicrafts, many of them imported from elsewhere in Mexico, relatively inexpensive by American standards. Ceramic figures and black pottery from Oaxaca, hammocks from the state of Yucatán, brightly painted balsa wood animals, blown glass, elaborate *huipiles* (women's sacklike dresses), mahogany carvings, and other regional handicrafts are finding their way to the shops of Cozumel. Black coral, shells and shell jewelry, and other reminders of Cozumel's Palancar Reef are abundant.

Mexican liquor and liquers are inexpensive and there are some delicious and unusual ones unique to Mexico. (*Xtabentún,* an anise and honey liquer of Maya extraction, is best when sipped after biting into a fresh slice of lime.) T-shirts, beach towels, visors, and other souvenirs extolling Cozumel's virtues are of course widely available.

Most of the stores are located in the central district, and prices are as a rule slightly cheaper here than in the gift shops of the beachfront hotels. Prices are often written in dollars, and you may begin to wonder why you exchanged yours for stacks of deflated pesos. Since the exchange rate in stores is usually lower than that given in banks, however, buying in pesos will usually save you some money. It is comforting to know, however, that the American dollar is almost universally accepted on the island. Most stores are closed on Sun.

Most boutiques cater to the standard souvenir trade, but a few are notable for their unique or sizeable selection. *La Concha,* on Avenida 5 Sur, a half block south of the plaza, has a carefully selected inventory of ceramics from craft-rich states such as Oaxaca and Michoacán, woven purses from Guatemala, delicate silver ornaments, and more, at reasonable prices. *Cinco Soles,* on the waterfront at the north end of town, has some intriguing ceramic and wooden figures and glassware, in addition to the standard fare. You'll see some fine jewelry and black coral at *El Arca de Noe* on the same street. The *Handicraft Market,* located at the southeast corner of the plaza, has probably the largest selection of handmade wares. *La Casita* at Avenida Rafael Melgar Norte 23 sells designer clothes and an interesting selection of crafts and leather goods.

For those interested in more practical items, *Aca Joe, Express, Guess,* and *Esprit,* all on the waterfront, carry chic casual and resort wear, and there is a *Ralph Lauren's Polo Shop* for those who long for back-home prices. For fashionable women's clothing, stop in at *Emma's Boutique,* Avenida Júarez 164. *Joyería Caribbean,* nexy to PAMA on the plaza and *Van Cleef's,* in the Plaza del Sol Mall on the main plaza, sell exquisite jewelery at extravagant prices. *Casablanca,* located at Avenida Rafael Melgar 3, across from the downtown pier, should not be missed, if only in order to gaze wistfully at the luxuriously presented jewelry, gems, statuary, and expensive Mexican crafts.

Orbi, at the corner of Avenida 3, is a good place to buy dime store items, but not much else. *PAMA* Department store, on the south side of the plaza, is the largest outlet for untaxed foreign goods. *Plaza Maya 2000,* across the street from the Fiesta Americana Sol Caribe Hotel, is Cozumel's newest shopping center.

NIGHTLIFE. Evenings start early on Cozumel, and after a day in the water, many people retire early as well. But for those who want to play at night, mingle with other travelers, show off their tans, dance, and celebrate their vacations, there are places to go and people to see. Nightlife here is sleepy compared to Cancún, although more discotheques are springing up all the time.

Discos and Bars

Amadeus, across the street from Villa Blanca just south of town, is an attractive new bar; it attracts sporty types who have spent the day in salt water.

Noche Pirata. A party boat that leaves from the downtown pier every evening at 6. Boasts all you can drink, live music, buffet dinner, and dancing. Returns at 10 P.M. Make reservations through your hotel travel desk.

Neptuno, on the Malecón at the corner of Calle 11 Sur. A diver's hangout, everyone here has a great tan, or at least a sunburned nose.

Scaramouche, on the corner of Avenida Rafael Melgar and Rosado Salas, is open every night until 3:30 A.M.

Carlos 'n Charlie's and Jimmy Kitchen, on the Malecón, has a far-reaching reputation as fun place with a good vacation atmosphere; it gets pretty rowdy and noisy late at night.

ISLA MUJERES

From Pirate Hideout to Resort

by
JIM BUDD

The name means Isle of Women, something of a misnomer these days. A Spanish expedition under the command of Francisco Hernández de Córdoba discovered the island in March, 1517, and came across an imposing temple empty of people but crowded with stone female figures. Thus they named the place Isla Mujeres.

There is some speculation that the island may have been a convent-like retreat for the sacred virgins of the Mayas, or perhaps a harem, but nobody can say with any certainty.

Once found, Isla Mujeres was quickly forgotten. For much of its history it was a hideout for pirates and later a tiny fishing community. There is a Mexican navy base here now, home port for the two or three destroyers that comprise the country's Caribbean fleet.

Presently Isla Mujeres is best known as the place the catamarans and motor yachts head on their picnic cruises from Cancún. But Isla Mujeres is a destination in its own right, and has been since long before Cancún was a gleam in anybody's eye. The island has

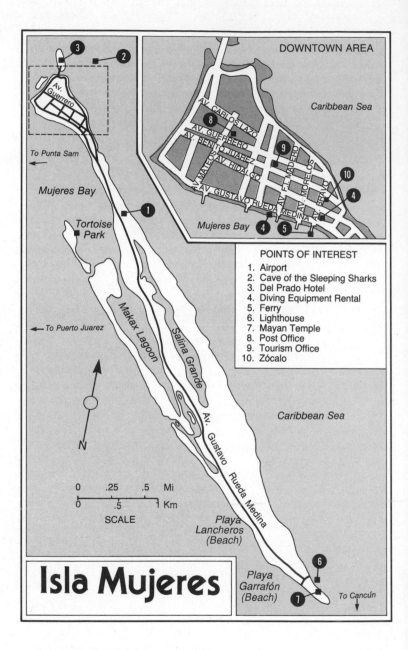

DOWNTOWN AREA

Caribbean Sea

Av. Guerrero

To Punta Sam

Mujeres Bay

Tortoise
Park

AV. CARLOS LAZO
AV. GUERRERO
AV. BENITO JUAREZ
AV. HIDALGO
AV. MATEO
AV. GUSTAVO RUEDA MEDINA
AV. F. MADERO
AV. MORELOS
BRAVO

Mujeres Bay

To Puerto Juarez

Makax Lagoon

Salina Grande

Av. Gustavo Rueda Medina

POINTS OF INTEREST

1. Airport
2. Cave of the Sleeping Sharks
3. Del Prado Hotel
4. Diving Equipment Rental
5. Ferry
6. Lighthouse
7. Mayan Temple
8. Post Office
9. Tourism Office
10. Zócalo

Caribbean Sea

N

0   .25   .5   Mi
0   .5   1 Km
SCALE

*Playa
Lancheros
(Beach)*

Isla Mujeres

*Playa
Garrafón
(Beach)*

To Cancún

its odd little hotels, along with one first-class establishment, quite a few delightful seafood restaurants, a handful of cute shops, and a surprising amount of night life.

Price is the big attraction. Isla Mujeres is cheap, the most laid-back resort area in the Mexican Caribbean. Backpackers and beachcomber types arrive prepared to stay as long as their money holds out, which may be for months. Those so inclined can charter cruisers for deep-sea fishing expeditions, go out scuba diving, snorkel many places right off shore, or hunt up a new place for a picnic. For many, however, Isla Mujeres is simply a place to forget the world, soak in the sun, read a few good books, and perhaps fall in love.

EXPLORING ISLA MUJERES

Five miles long, perhaps half-a-mile wide at its waist, with one village at its northern end, Isla Mujeres is not much more than a palm-fringed sandbar. Although almost a third of the island is taken up by an airport, scheduled air service is not always available. Almost everyone who comes to stay (as opposed to day-trippers on picnic cruises) arrives by ferry from Puerto Juárez, which is just outside Cancún City.

The ferries make the three-mile crossing in about an hour, putting into a dock along the Malecón, the waterfront avenue. The little town here is about three blocks wide and maybe ten blocks long. The *zócalo,* or main square, is two blocks up, or inland, from the ferry dock.

Taxis are available for travelers with luggage heading for a hotel. Anyone else will simply want to wander the sandy little streets, poking into the tiny shops, and checking out the looks of the restaurants.

Cocos Beach is at the far end of the Malecón, just beyond the village near the northern tip of the island. The other beach up at this end is Pancholo, looking out on the open Caribbean. Lovely to look at, this is no place to swim; the current is rough and dangerous.

For those who will be staying awhile, the village has about all Isla Mujeres has to offer. The Malecón is the place, for instance, to charter a fishing boat or arrange a scuba diving trip. This is where the hotels, shops and most of the restaurants are.

Getting around the island means taking a taxi or renting a moped scooter. No rental cars are available on Isla Mujeres. They can be brought over on the car ferry that departs from Punta Sam—beyond Puerto Juárez on the mainland—but this scarcely seems worth the effort.

Mopeds are inexpensive. Credit cards are taken for deposit, but actual payment must be made in cash. It's important to take time to learn how these contraptions work, especially how to start them once they are stopped, and how to shift gears. Caution also is important. Careless riders may take some nasty tumbles, and you ride a moped strictly at your own risk.

A nice ride is along the road that huddles on the seaward side of the island. Beyond the airport, it is a long empty stretch for a couple of miles and the civilized world seems far, far away.

Pirate Home a Highlight

Eventually this road turns inland, as it were, passing by one of Isla Mujeres' most famous sites, the home of Mundaca the Pirate.

Fermin Mundaca was, at the beginning of the nineteenth century, the island's most notorious resident. He was more of a slaver than buccaneer, but pirating sounds more dashing. The love of a good woman almost reformed him.

The señorita who captured Mundaca's heart wanted no truck with a slaver. Pledging to turn over a new leaf, our hero built a palatial home on the island, hoping it would be presided over by the girl he wished to make his bride. That was not to be. The young woman ran off with some poor but honorable fellow and Mundaca, broken hearted, lived out his days in Mérida. His mansion is now a ruin.

Past Mundaca's estate, the road joins the leeward highway that runs to the southern tip of the island where a lighthouse towers and one can find the remains of the lone Maya temple that still stands on Isla Mujeres.

El Garrafón

Out this way is El Garrafón (The Jug), the beach at which the picnic cruise boats from Cancún put in.

El Garrafón is a national park, most of it underwater, for tropical fish are the big attraction. The sand here eases off into a reef, home of parrot fish, angelfish, blueheads, sergeant majors, and any number of other colorful sea creatures. Snorkeling is the way to see them and gear is available for rent. There are a number of restaurants out this way, too.

Less than a mile up the coast is Lancheros Beach with its turtle pens, where you can catch a ride on the back of a giant turtle.

A little farther along is a turn off to the bridge that leads across the Makax Lagoon and out to Treasure Island. Treasure Island is something of a small theme park complete with a shipwreck, sunken galleon, open-air theater, and lots of shops and restaurants. Most of its customers are day-trippers from Cancún.

The main road runs along the shore of the lagoon where, it is said, long before poor Mundaca, more swashbuckling corsairs anchored their ships or lay in wait for victims along the Spanish Main. The handsome airstrip that covers so much of the island was put in by U–boat hunters during World War II.

From here the road runs back through town and all the way out to the Hotel Del Prado, which stands apart on its own little island and is the only first-class hostelry on Isla Mujeres.

Exploring, for most vacationers, also includes a few boat trips. One of the most popular is to Contoy, an island bird sanctuary, home of cranes, ducks, pelicans, and countless other species. The voyage, nearly three hours each way, includes a picnic on the uninhabited island.

Braving the Sharks

Scuba diving expeditions from Isla Mujeres are not quite as spectacular as those from Cozumel, but they can include an experience not soon forgotten—a visit to the Cave of the Sleeping Sharks.

Sharks, it is said, never sleep, which, as one wag noted, may account for their nasty dispositions. These fish must keep moving to force water through their gills. In the underwater caves off Isla Mujeres, however, fresh water bubbles up from a spring and creates something of a current of its own. Sharks, many of them big brutes, find their way into these grottoes and flake out. Certified scuba divers, some of them anyway, enjoy swimming among these beasts, even caressing them. As far as is known, all divers have returned unharmed.

Sporting types who prefer to keep to the surface can arrange to go deep-sea fishing from Isla Mujeres. Spring and early summer is the time to go after billfish. The rest of the year barracuda and tuna are caught.

Nightlife on Isla Mujeres has been described as sitting on the beach and watching the sun go down. In reality it can be a trifle more exciting than that. People often eat late and linger over their dinner. There are some nice little restaurants in town and even a lobster dinner is reasonably priced. There are also a few discos, plus a lone cinema that occasionally shows a flick from Hollywood.

Few vacationers on Isla Mujeres, however, seem much concerned about keeping busy. Doing nothing, relaxing after that, taking a siesta, and then getting back to doing nothing can be a fine way to watch the days slip by. For a change of pace, Cancún is only a boatride away, and even the Maya ruins at Tulum can be visited in a day.

PRACTICAL INFORMATION FOR ISLA MUJERES

HOW TO GET THERE. Most international travelers fly into Cancún, get themselves downtown aboard an airport minibus, and then taxi over to Puerto Juárez which is where ferries depart for the island. These boats usually leave every hour on the half-hour, 8:30 A.M.–7:30 P.M., although schedules are not adhered to regularly. A car ferry leaves Punta Sam—

about five miles north of Puerto Juárez—every two hours from 7 A.M. to 10 P.M. Passengers on the Punta Sam ferry pay less than 50¢. Another quicker way to get to Isla Mujeres is the water taxi operated by the Isla Mujeres *Cooperativa* from 7:30 A.M. to 8 P.M. for $5.

TELEPHONES. The area code for Isla Mujeres is 988; to call from the United States first dial 01152. Long-distance calls from the island must be made with operator assistance; because of taxes, collect calls are much less expensive.

ACCOMMODATIONS. With one exception, the hotels on Isla Mujeres are either *Moderate* ($35–100) or *Inexpensive* (under $35), and their rates are even lower between May and mid-Dec. The Del Prado, the island's only *Expensive* ($100 and up) property, was badly damaged by Hurricane Gilbert but is now fully operational.

Expensive

Del Prado Isla Mujeres. Punta Norte; 2 0122. A seven-story landmark on its own little islet, this resort has air-conditioned rooms, a pool, Windsurfing, sailing, and a dive shop plus entertainment at night.

Moderate

Maria's Kan Kin. Playa Garrafón; 3 1420. Out by Garrafón Beach. This is the island's best restaurant and now has 8 rooms or suites and 1 palapa-style bungalow.

Perla del Caribe. Madero 2; 2 0444. Also out on the seaward side, this is a fairly new hotel. All of its 94 rooms are air-conditioned; 34 rooms have terraces. Restaurant and bar.

Inexpensive

Berny. Juarez y Abasolo, 2 0025. About a block up from the ferry terminal and the beach. Its 37 rooms have fans. Bar and restaurant.

Caribe Maya. Madero 9; 2 0190. Small, clean, and in the heart of the village. 6 of the 21 rooms have air-conditioning.

Poc-Na. Calle Matamozos; 2 0090. In town, this is a hostel with dorms for men and women, a choice of hammocks or beds (sheets cost extra), plus an inexpensive dining room open for breakfast, lunch, and dinner.

Rocamar. Avenida Nicolás Bravo and Guerrero; 2 0101. On the seaward side of the island on a rocky point. Close to town with 32 fan-cooled terraced rooms, this is a friendly place with a restaurant.

DINING OUT. Many people visit Isla Mujeres simply to have lunch. For those staying on the island, dinner often is the high spot of the day. Menus are pretty much limited to seafood. Here we classify any place charging $15 or more for a meal as *Expensive,* around $10 as *Moderate,* and *Inexpensive* those where a meal should not cost more than $6. Drinks and tips are extra. Unless otherwise noted, all these restaurants are open for breakfast, lunch, and dinner. As for credit cards, AE is American Express; MC, MasterCard; V, Visa.

Expensive

Ciro's. A lobster house just up the street from the docks (2 0102). Steak is on the menu, too. No breakfast. MC, V.

Gomar. 2 blocks from the waterfront (2 0142); Steaks and seafood are the draw here. Quite romantic; open evenings only. AE, MC, V.

Maria's Kan Kin. At Garrafón Beach (3 1420); reason enough to visit Isla Mujeres. The peppered turtle steak and the lobster parisienne are favorites, as is rabbit stew. MC, V.

El Peregrino. Downtown. Regarded by locals as the best restaurant on the island. Steak and seafood are the house specialties.

Moderate

Buho's. On the beach at the northern end of town; serves steak as well as lobster. Disco music later in the evening. AE, MC, V.

El Garrafón and **Garrafón de Castilla.** The two best restaurants out by Garrafón Beach. Both specialize in seafood and are open only for lunch. MC, V.

Villa del Mar. On the Malecón across from the docks; convenient and good. It is especially nice for breakfast. MC, V.

Inexpensive

Guillermo's. A block from the docks; a soda fountain sort of place serving snacks and complete meals.

Pizza Rolandi. Calle Hidalgo between Madero and Abasolo. Open daily for pizza and pastas.

HOW TO GET AROUND. The choice is either by **taxi** or a rented **moped scooter.** Since the island is only 5 miles long, taxi fares rarely hit $3. Mopeds rent for $20 per day or $7 for two hours; credit cards are taken as a deposit, but payment must be made in cash. Prior to renting a scooter, take time to learn how it works, especially how to start it and how to shift gears. And be careful! Accidents can happen, and in these parts you will have to pay your own medical expenses. There are several moped renters within a block or two of the ferry dock.

TOURIST INFORMATION. The state tourist bureau (2 0188) maintains an office on the main plaza (*zócalo*) about two blocks from the ferry dock. Personnel are quite helpful and will assist in trying to find a room.

BEACHES. *Coco Beach,* north of town on the island's leeward side, is one of the nicest places to swim along the entire Mexican Caribbean.

Pancholo Beach, while also close to town, looks out on the open sea and is a dangerous place for swimming. But for picnicking, holding hands, and soaking up the sun, it is lovely.

Lancheros Beach, near the southern end of the island, is noted for its turtle pens, the catching and canning of sea turtles being one of the major activities on the island. There are a handful of seafood shacks here and musicians often play during the afternoon.

El Garrafón, close to the southern tip of the island, is a national park, famed for the tropical fish that congregate near the reefs offshore. This is where the cruise boats from Cancún put in. Snorkeling is superb here and gear is available for rent. Three of the island's better restaurants are out this way.

Treasure Island is a seaside theme park that lies along the peninsula east of Makax Lagoon. It is a good place to snorkel or actually ride a turtle, and there are a number of shops here along with a restaurant.

BABY-SITTING SERVICES. Given sufficient time, even the smallest hotels can arrange for someone to keep a tot company. Few sitters, however, speak English.

SPORTS. Deep-sea fishing. Charters can be arranged for about $350 for 4 chairs at the *Sociedad Cooperativa* (2 0274), the boatmen's cooperative by the docks; price depends upon the size of the boat to be taken out. Billfishing is best during late spring and early summer. Barracuda and tuna, both good fighters, bite all through the year. Fishing outings often include trips to uninhabited Contoy Island for a seafood barbecue.

Scuba diving, while not as spectacular as off Cozumel, can be quite good from Isla Mujeres. Special is a trip to the Cave of the Sleeping Sharks, an undersea grotto where fresh water bubbles up from a spring, allowing the sharks to snooze. It is, to say the least, a memorable experience, but one open only to certified divers. The *Hotel Del Prado's* sport desk (2 0122), *Sociedad Cooperativa,* and the adjacent *Mexico Divers* make dive trips and offer both brief resort courses ($50) and full certification programs (which take up to a week and cost $365). A 2-tank dive trip from Isla Mujeres costs about $60.

Snorkeling requires no special training although those donning mask and flippers for the first time will need to flop around a bit before they get the hang of it. Gear is available for rent at several shops around town as well as at Garrafón Beach, where the snorkeling is spectacular. Usual price is $15 for a 3½- to 4-hour trip. Snorkeling trips to Contoy Island, including a grilled fish lunch on the beach cost $30 for a day trip.

HISTORIC SITES. The ruined Maya temple on the southern tip of the island was literally blown away by Hurricane Gilbert in 1988. Now the island's only ruin is the Mundaca estate near Lancheros Beach. It was built as a grand mansion by Fermin Mundaca, an early 19th-century pirate and slaver who hoped to impress his lady love. The girl in question preferred someone with a less shady past and Mundaca abandoned his showplace to the jungle.

SHOPPING. Though the selection is uninspired, most of the basics are available at the islands many shops. Since the streets are unblemished by signs, addresses would be meaningless. *Farmacia Isla Mujeres,* near the plaza, sells everything from film and tanning lotion to pills and ointment. *Super Betino,* also near the plaza, carries food and drink for those who would dine in their rooms, plus sportswear and cosmetics. *Casa del Arte* is a good place to pick up rubbings from Maya temples along with jewelry and handicrafts. *La Playita* and *Poco Loco,* on the Malecón, have what may be the island's best selection of resort wear.

NIGHTLIFE. Surprisingly, Isla Mujeres offers a fair amount of action after dark, including an occasional movie in English shown at the town's one cinema.

Most of the restaurant bars feature a happy hour from 5 until 7 P.M. The *Villa del Mar,* Avenida Rueda Medina, is a favorite gathering place. Discos include *Bronco,* Avenida Nicolás, Bravo 6 (2 0062); *Buho's,* Aveni-

da Carlos, Lazo 1 (2 0179); and *Tequila,* Avenida Matamoros (2 0019).
Buho's and *Tequila* are usually the most lively.

MEXICO'S CARIBBEAN COAST

A Wilderness Bordering Luxury

by
MARIBETH MELLIN

A former senior editor of San Diego *Magazine, Maribeth Mellin is a San Diego–based freelance writer who works for the Copley News Service. She has been making regular forays to Mexico for the past 10 years.*

While Cancún and Cozumel are Mexico's Caribbean resorts, the coastline of mainland Quintana Roo is Mexico's Caribbean wilderness, with a few luxurious lagoons, even fewer tourist traps, and an endless dose of paradise. Quintana Roo didn't gain statehood until 1974, and though most people refer to the Caribbean coast as Yucatán, it is really all part of Quintana Roo.

The northern part of the state, including Cancún, is heavily influenced by its proximity to the State of Yucatán. The music, food and cultural traditions are Yucatecan. The Mexican Government's decision to transform Cancún into a world-class resort has brought an international flare to the region, where continental restaurants and exotic boutiques flourish just a few miles from small Maya villages. The center is more purely Maya, with small seaside fishing collectives and jungle and coastal neighborhoods where the close-knit Maya residents carry on ancient traditions. The south, particularly Chetumal, is influenced by its status as a port area adjacent to Guatemala and Belize. The ethnic mix of Maya, other Central Americans, Middle Easterners, and blacks affects the food and calypso and reggae music.

Though buses do connect these regions and are popular with backpackers, a rental car or Jeep allows you to explore more thoroughly and creatively without ending up alone in the jungle after dark or in the rain. Huge *Mayarama* tour buses from resort hotels in Cancún appear regularly at the ruins, parks, and beaches with their loads of sightseers who bolster local economies.

Highway 307 is the only paved road running north–south along coastal Quintana Roo. The 215-mile route from Cancún to Chetumal hugs the coast up to the ruins at Tulum; then it swings inward to Felipe Carrillo Puerto, once called Chan Santa Cruz; finally it cuts through the jungle to the bays and lagoons at Chetumal. The entrances to ruins, resorts, beaches, and campgrounds are marked with an assortment of road signs, ranging from billboards to painted tires hanging from wooden posts. Each year there are more picture-coded tourist signs, pointing the way to restaurants, gas stations, and hotels. Roads and paths, some seemingly impassable, branch off Highway 307 through the short, dense jungle, leading to adventures five or ten kilometers away.

Where Wildlife Wander

Along the more civilized routes wild pigs, oscillating turkeys, monkeys, iguanas, lizards, and snakes (including the notoriously poisonous, four-nosed *nahuyaca*) appear in the clearings. *Balam* (the jaguar), *ceh* (the stag), armadillos, tapir, wild boar, peccaries, ocelots, raccoons, and badgers all inhabit the dense, uncivilized jungle. Alligators, giant turtles, sharks, barracuda, and manatee seacows inhabit the reefs, lagoons, cenotes, and caves along the Caribbean and down the Hondo River, which runs along the borders between Mexico, Belize, and Guatemala. During July and August, tourists along the mainland coast witness the annual spectacle of sea turtles laying thousands of eggs on the beach. Many of those leathery eggs are harvested and sold as delicacies in Cancún and Mérida. Those that remain hatch in the night, and the sight of tiny turtle hatchlings fleeing to the sea is an unusual delight.

Coastal Quintana Roo attracts scuba divers and snorkelers to transparent turquoise and emerald waters strewn with rose, black, and red coral reefs and sunken pirate ships. Schools of black, gray, and gold angelfish, sparkling green and purple parrotfish, earth-toned manta rays, and scores of other jewel-toned tropical species seem oblivious to the clicking underwater cameras. The visibility in these waters reaches over 100 feet; it's not unusual to get a sampling of the underwater scene without even getting wet.

Birdwatchers stare into the jungle for a rare glimpse of parrots, toucans, and the long red and green feathers of the sacred quetzal. Amateurs are entertained by yellow, blue, and scarlet butterflies, singing cicadas and orioles, sparkling dragonflies, kite-like frigates, and night owls nesting in the trees. Colorless crabs scuttle sideways toward the coconut groves over pale, white limestone and sand that never burns the soles of your feet. Tiny mosquitoes and gnats, impervious to mild repellents, bore through the smallest rips in window screens, tents, and mosquito nets and crave the blood of tourists. Always carry and use strong repellent if you react to such bites. Some say the bugs won't bother you if you take large doses of Vitamin B1 for a few weeks or months before your trip.

Mayan Influence

The Caribbean Coast is Mayan. Spanish is frequently spoken and understood, but most of the towns, ranches, and coastal settlements have Maya names which the residents pronounce like no one else, with the clicks and slurs of the Maya language. Many of the maps handed out by rental and tourist agencies list towns and lagoons with a variety of spellings and have a tendency to misplace bays and lagoons. The 60-mile stretch between Cancún and Tulum boasts more and more signs with kilometer readings that help clarify the confusion. Wrong turns are no problem—they may lead you to private beaches and coves or barely discernible ruins that add to your Mayan adventure.

Puerto Morelos, Playa del Carmen, Felipe Carrillo Puerto, and Chetumal are the only major stops along the way where one can find groceries, sundries, banks, telephone offices, and auto supplies. Electricity and telephones are the exception rather than the rule, but most resorts have radio communication with the outside world. Incongruities such as the sound of Ozzie and Harriet Nelson beamed in by satellite to a hotel TV add to the magical charm of this remote region on the verge of discovery.

Puerto Morelos

Puerto Morelos, a small coastal town that sports a few more streets, hotels, and homes each year, is about 20 miles from Cancún. A Pemex station and tourist signs mark the crossroads, and most shops, banks, and businesses are clustered around the central square and playground. Large cruise ships, buses, and small planes stop in town regularly. The car-and-people ferries sail to Cozumel from a long pier south of the square. Large trucks, RVs, Jeeps, and Volkswagen bugs line up hours before the ferry departs, supposedly twice a day. The fare is low—about $2 per person, $7.50 for autos, $15 for RVs; there is a Pemex station by the pier.

Thus far, there are no major car rental offices in Puerto Morelos. This creates a bit of a problem because you cannot take your rental car to the island on the ferry and leave it there. Cars must be returned in Cancún or Chetumal.

The two mainstay resorts, La Ceiba and Playa Ojo de Agua, were badly damaged by Hurricane Gilbert in October 1988. When operating, these resorts cater to dive groups, and they have dive shops, tours, equipment, and classes. The restaurants are quite good. Three lighthouses from different historical periods break up the long stretch of beach, which rarely feels crowded.

Punta Bete

A four-mile-long white, sandy beach between rocky lagoons, just 500 yards from Lafitte Reef, provides the setting for two unusual resorts created by an enterprising American named Arnold Bilgore. The bungalow lifestyle of Capitán Lafitte's and the luxury camping at Kailuum draw a steady clientele of returnees and friends who discover their brand of paradise by word of mouth. Bilgore's resort empire has spread to Shangri-La at Playa del Carmen and a proposed divers' resort on an island off Belize. Water sports, gourmet dining, congenial conversation, and hammock relaxation are Bilgore's version of vacationing; the concept is carried on by his son and daughter, who manage Kailuum. The cabins are about five kilometers down a dirt road; taxis bring travelers from the buses, ferries, and planes in Playa del Carmen. Other hotels and campgrounds occupy the Punta Bete beach less than five kilometers south. Except for the lights from the cruise ships and the shoreline of Cozumel, there is no sign of outer civilization.

Playa del Carmen

Playa del Carmen is the busiest and most tourist-oriented town between Cancún and Chetumal. Cruise ships and tour buses regularly discharge passengers to the strip of crafts stands leading to the pier, where the passenger-only ferry to Cozumel departs approximately every two hours. Planes to Cozumel leave hourly during daylight from the airstrip just off Highway 307. The bus depot is a large fenced parking lot in the middle of town; buses depart for Cancún and Chetumal and spots in between regularly. Boys with bicycle carts patrol the route between the various transportation points, carrying travelers' luggage and purchases.

The beaches at Playa del Carmen are crystalline white, despite all the boat and people traffic, and the water is a brilliant shade of blue that photographs beautifully. Windsailers, snorklers, swimmers, and sunbathers dot the long waterfront. Transportation to ruins, parks, and other beaches is readily available. Doctors, ambulances, and *farmacias* are readily available; shops carry most necessary items, including fan belts, batteries, and the essential mosquito repellent. The long-distance telephone is located in a storefront just off the main plaza, under the orange and white tower.

Prices for meals and rooms in Playa del Carmen are a bit higher than on the rest of the coast, but the location is ideal for day trips to ruins and parks.

Xcaret

The dirt road to Xcaret ends at a small shack, where tourists pay a token fee (less than 50 cents) to visit the small clearing of Mayan shrines, still under excavation. The lagoons here are particularly nice for divers who can spend hours swimming through caves filled with spring water and around rocky inlets where the mix of fresh and seawater creates an unusual blend of greens and blues. Slightly north of the most popular diving area is a sacred cenote and Mayan altar.

Paamul

This crescent-shaped lagoon has choice snorkeling because a coral reef protects its mouth, leaving the waters placid and clear. The reef is easily reached by the average swimmer. A jungle path to the north leads to a lagoon four times the size of the first, and even more private. Trailer camps, cabanas, and tent camps are scattered along the beach, with one major restaurant selling cold beer and fresh fish. The beaches are better than most for beach-combers, who find shells, sand dollars, and even glass beads washed to the shore from the sunken pirate ships at Akumal. Paamul is a good spot for watching the sea turtle hatchlings in the late summer. There is a small fishing community called Xpuha nine kilometers south on a narrow path where residents weave hammocks and harvest coconuts. There are a few small overgrown ruin sites in the area with traces of painting on the inside walls. Just south of Paamul is Playa Aventuras, a government-owned camp for Mexican children.

Akumal

Akumal, 22 miles south of Playa del Carmen, means "Place of the Turtle," and before it became a major resort the beach was littered with thousands of turtle eggs. The area first drew attention in 1926 when explorers discovered the *Mantanceros*, a Spanish galleon that sank in 1741. The area is rich in history, and is said to be the burial site for the famed pirate Jean Lafitte. Akumal first became a headquarters for the Mexican Underwater Explorers Club and a resort for wealthy underwater adventurers who flew into the area on small private planes and searched the waters for sunken treasures. A resort building boom of sorts has taken place in the past few years, and now there are three large condominium and hotel resorts, all ever-expanding.

The long curved bay and beach is rarely empty; most times it resembles the beaches along Cancún, with rows of glamorous sunbathers and swimmers. There is a small marine museum on the grounds of the Akumal Club Caribe, with exhibits of treasures from the sunken galleons just off the coast. Another underwater museum gives snorkelers and divers the chance to examine the wreckage.

Akumal gets crowded and busy at times, particularly when the tour buses to Tulum stop here for lunch, and it is most popular for those who want a resort with all the comforts of Cancún without the highrises.

Chemuyil

The sign at the intersection on Highway 307 calls Chemuyil "The Most Beautiful Beach in the World." The author's enthusiasm is understandable. Chemuyil is one of those idyllic settings that would delight an adventurous couple on their honeymoon. There isn't a tour bus in sight, not even a hotel. Just a long white beach and coconut grove with a few dome tents hiding behind the tree trunks and colorful hammocks swinging in the shade. The bar–restaurant is a round palapa with your choice of seats—bar stools or hammocks. A small shop offers rental equipment, bathing suits, and T-shirts. Private palapas with mosquito net sides, a center round table and two hammocks can be rented for overnight or just as a shady resting spot during a day at the beach. Some say the snorkeling here is the best on the coast; the series of coves are like private aquariums.

Chemuyil is gaining attention as a resort site. Thus far, there is one luxurious white villa on the northernmost cove, but there are plans for luxury homes and condos in the area.

Xcacel

The restaurant at this lagoon sits up on a sandy ridge overlooking yet another long white beach. There is a usage fee, and camping is allowed, but the restaurant is closed on Sundays. Some Mayarama buses stop here in the afternoon, and the showers and dressing rooms get crowded as the day ends.

Xel-Ha

Xel-Ha, a natural aquarium cut out of the limestone shoreline, is a natural park and breeding center for countless species of tropical fish. Several lagoons are connected to each other by underwater currents; the rocky coastline curves into bays and coves where enormous parrotfish cluster around an underwater Mayan shrine. Another shrine marks the entrance to the park; gift shops and food stands line the parking lot. As you enter the grounds, you pass a large underwater preserve where swimming is prohibited. When the water is perfectly clear, it is possible to see giant stingrays and nurse sharks swimming about. There is a good restaurant at the water's edge, and rental shops with diving and snorkeling gear and underwater cameras. Glass bottom boats traverse the water's edge.

Xel-Ha can get incredibly crowded at the peak of the tourist season, when buses unload hundreds of tourists from Cancún. Many of these sightseers stay out of the water, watching the action from the rocky shoreline. Fortunately, the lagoons are very large, and it is possible to swim far enough out to snorkel alone and stare back at the lineup of oglers on the shore. Though the waters here are not as clear as they once were, Xel-Ha is still an excellent snorkeling spot as the fish are free to breed and survive, protected against fishing lines, spears, and nets. There is a small entrance fee, and the park is open from 9 A.M. to 5 P.M.

Tulum

Of all the Mayan ruins, Tulum is perhaps the most enchanting, perched on a cliff overlooking the Caribbean sea. The ruin site is about eight miles south of Xel-Ha, near the intersection of the road running west to the jungle ruins of Cobá. There are a few restaurants and small, rundown hotels at the Highway 307 intersection with the road to the ruins, and buses stop regularly there. Souvenir and handicraft stands surround the large parking lot at the ruins, and small stands sell soda and snacks. The ruin site itself is small but scenic. (See the chapter on *Exploring the Maya Country* for descriptions of the structures.) Tulum has many diehard devotees, who swear the ruins hold a magical enchantment that captivates them. There is a small beach below the ruin site, but no showers or dressing rooms. The ruins are open from 9 A.M. to 5 P.M., and are guarded at night.

Tulum is located at a natural break in the chain of reefs running alongside the coastline. A lighthouse near the ruins guides boats through the reefs to the shore. At the south end of the parking lot, a paved road travels for four and a half miles past small campgrounds, hotels, and fishing collectives. The pavement ends at a beautiful large cove and coconut grove where the road sign reads *Cuida Su Vida, No Se Distraiga* ("For Your Life, Don't Get Distracted"). Just south of it is Sian Ka, an underwater and terrestrial preserve. The dirt road from there runs through 35 kilometers of beaches and jungles; the road is narrow and rough. More campgrounds, hotels, restaurants, luxury villas, and deserted palapas dot the dense jungle along the road, which grows ever more narrow as it heads toward the small resort of Villa de Boca Paila, a fishing resort, and Punta Allen, a small lobstering town. Travelers with reservations here are normally picked up at the Cozumel airport and flown by seaplane to the point. This remote region is popular with sportfisherman because of the elusive, fast-swimming bonefish that populate the waters there.

The tiny pueblo of Tulum is about four kilometers south of the ruins off Highway 307; it cannot be reached from the road to Punta Allen. The town does little to encourage tourism, and is really a small, poor community with one market, a butcher shop, a taco stand, and a small central square where pigs and dogs roam free. There is a lot of building going on along the highway, though, and Tulum could soon lose its anonymity and become a major resort.

Felipe Carillo Puerto

Highway 307 intersects with Highway 184 at Felipe Carillo Puerto. The trip on Highway 184 to Mérida is about 175 miles through jungle, ranches, and small settlements. Felipe Carillo Puerto's main claim to fame is the role it played in the 1850s during the War of the Castes. The Maya at that time believed in "talking idols," so those living in Chan Santa Cruz were not surprised when voices rose from the mahogany cross in the main church. The voices urged the people to create a new religion and go to war. Government troops arrived and killed the ventriloquist who spoke through the cross from a curtained chamber. The cross was destroyed during a battle. In the 1860s, the Indians began building a monumental temple of stone and mortar, which was never completed. The base of this temple still sits in Felipe Carrillo as a monument to the War of the Castes. There isn't much else to explore in this town, except the branch office of the Instituto Nacional Indigenista, a federal agency that helps Indians living in small jungle settlements adapt to modern times. Highway 307 south from here travels through jungle inhabited by jaguars, boar, deer, and a few Indians.

Chetumal

Chetumal, the last Mexican town on the southern Caribbean, is 245 miles southeast of Mérida and 235 miles south of Cancún. Devastated by a hurricane in 1955, Chetumal was rebuilt into a modern port city and appears newer and cleaner than most ports. The city was once a center of religious power. Now it is the capital of the state of Quintana Roo, which was originally a part of Yucatán and then a federal territory until 1974, when it gained statehood. Chetumal is visited by Mexican and Belizian travelers because of its status as a free port and major center for imported goods. There is an airport with flights to Mérida and Cancún. Buses depart to other points in Mexico and Belize. *Avis,* located at the *Del Prado,* and several local agencies rent cars and Jeeps. If you are renting a car elsewhere and plan to drop it off in Chetumal, be sure your agency has a branch there.

Chetumal is sometimes called "The City of the Red Soul"; in Mayan its name was *Chactemal,* meaning "where the red-woods (or dye sticks) grow," referring to the *chacte* tree from which a red pigment is extracted. The port, located on the Bahía Chetumal, is a major shipping center for the hardwoods, such as mahogany, grown in the jungles. Many of the buildings and homes are built with red-hued mahogany and cedar and yellow sapodilla and have red tin roofs that glow in the light of the rising and setting sun. Most buildings are one story, with a few modern three-story government buildings and hotels. The wide Bahía Boulevard, lined with monuments and an old lighthouse, runs along the waterfront. The boulevard is a popular gathering spot at night.

Chetumal is a free port and a haven for smugglers. For years there was no practical way to ship Mexican goods into Quintana Roo and imports were exempted from taxes. Many items still are sold tax-free, and travelers heading into Yucatán or other parts of Mexico must first clear customs. The shops lining Avenida Heroes continue to sell goods that cannot be found elsewhere in Mexico, and the intrigue of the old days still hangs in the air. The smuggling trade still survives all attempts to quelch it.

Chetumal is Mayan, but has a mixed population with Caribbean influences. The music tends more toward calypso than mariachi, and there are communities of blacks and Middle Easterners who add an exotic flare to the city life. The food is also a mix of Yucatécan, Mexican, and Middle Eastern, and the most common dish is beans and rice with chicken, vegetables, and coconut milk. The traditional dish *tikinchic* includes grilled fish, rice seasoned with sour-orange juice, and achiote sauce.

Chetumal's proximity to Belize (formerly called British Honduras) adds to the mystique. The cities in Belize are not nearly as clean and orderly, and a sense of danger fills the air as the government of Belize establishes itself as an independent country, with some help from British troops still stationed there as a safeguard against the Guatemalans, who consider Belize to be their territory. Travelers who wish to visit Belize must pass through customs at the border, and leave their rental cars in Chetumal. Rickety buses with wooden benches lining the sides depart from the border for Corozal and Orange Walk. Day visitors should stick with Corozal, only ten miles inside the border, where they can get a good shrimp lunch at Tony's Motel and a fair sense of the wildness of Belize.

Chetumal's bayfront beaches are as clean and white as those along the coast. Calderitas, five miles north of town, has the best swimming, and divers frequent Chinchorro, an atoll reef two hours offshore and littered with shipwrecks. Chetumal's major water attractions, however, sit farther inland. The Hondo River runs between Chetumal, Belize, and Guatemala. In its wildest parts alligators roam the riverbeds and manatees, or sea cows, breed. The Palmar and Obregon springs by the river just outside Chetumal have rustic resorts. Cenote Azul, a huge well 200 meters in diameter, is on the edge of Bacalar Lagoon. It gets its name from its clear blue waters, with visibility of 80 meters or more. The cenote is surrounded by lush vegetation; the underwater caves are popular with divers. Laguna Milagros, 14 kilometers from Chetumal, is a lovely lagoon with a center island and a shoreline surrounded by palms and blooming bouganvilla, but most travelers prefer to go 22 kilometers to Laguna de Bacalar.

Bacalar is known as the lagoon of seven colors. As the sea and fresh waters mix, the shades of green and blue intensify, and the border of dark jungle growth contrasts starkly with the clear waters. Water sports of all sorts are popular here. There are a few rustic hotels and campgrounds in the village of Bacalar and Xul-Ha on the southern tip of the lagoon. Restaurants and rental shops line the shores of the lagoon. Fuerte de Bacalar, a Spanish fort built in 1733 to ward off pirates, became a Maya stronghold during the Caste Wars, and it now holds some government offices and a museum. It is a pretty place for a picnic lunch among the colorful flower gardens.

Forty-five miles west of Chetumal off Highway 186 lies one of the more recently discovered ruins of Kohunlich with its Pyramid of the Masks portraying the Maya sun god, and one of the oldest ball courts in Quintana Roo.

PRACTICAL INFORMATION FOR
THE CARIBBEAN COAST

HOW TO GET THERE. Most travelers get to the Caribbean coast by way of Mérida, Cancún, Cozumel, or Chetumal. These cities can be reached by air, bus, or rental car, but there are restrictions with each mode.

By Air. *Aeroméxico, Mexicana,* and many major U.S. carriers fly to the above mentioned cities. *Aerocaribe* and *Aerocozumel* (both under the same management) link Cozumel, Cancún, Oaxaca, Veracruz, Villahermosa, Mérida and Playa del Carmen. Air Taxi service is available to many remote resort hotels and to the ruins at Cobá and Chichén Itzá.

By Car. Driving is the best way to take advantage of all the Yucatán coast has to offer because many of the mainland's scenic spots are a ways off the main highway, down dirt roads. Volkswagen Beetles, Rabbits, and Jeeps and similar types of vehicles are available at the cities mentioned above, from major rental companies such as *Hertz, Budget, Avis, Dollar,* and local companies. But there are some hassles. If you rent your car in Mérida and drive to the coast, you will be crossing state lines, from Yucatán into Quintana Roo. Be sure your company allows this, and discuss the drop-off charge, which is determined by how far apart your place of departure and destination are. For example, the charge to rent a car in Mérida and drop it off in Cancún is about $60. Be sure to get insurance. If Cozumel is on your itinerary, you will have to drop your car off on the mainland, since you may not take rental cars onto the island from the mainland (though rental cars are available on Cozumel). This situation complicates things as there are currently no car rental companies in Playa del Carmen or Puerto Morelos, where the ferries for Cozumel depart from. Your best bet is to return your car at the Cancún airport and fly to Cozumel on one of the commuter airlines (less than $10 per person).

By Bus. Mexico's invincible bus system reaches the edges of the coast, with major stops at Cancún, Puerto Morelos, Playa del Carmen, Felipe Carrillo Puerto, and Chetumal. The schedules are ever-changing, though you should be able to get some idea of time parameters at these major stops. While the first-class buses stop only at major points, the second-class buses seem to stop anywhere you want them to on their routes down Hwy. 307, but these stops can be 5 or 10 kms from your destination. Those traveling the coast by bus are advised to have strong walking shoes, lightweight baggage, and a flashlight.

TELEPHONES. Telephones are few and far between on the Caribbean Coast. There's no problem in Cancún or Chetumal, but in between, you must rely on the *larga distancia* offices (or storefronts) in Puerto Morelos, Playa del Carmen, and Felipe Carrillo Puerto. The phones are usually open from 9 A.M. until noon or so, and again in the early evening on weekdays. An operator will collect your money and patch your call through, while lines of people patiently await the end of your conversation. The connections are often poor.

ACCOMMODATIONS. One of the coast's most charming features is its wide range of resorts, hotels, and campgrounds, some of which come and go with the rains. The resorts are often geared to divers or fishermen; the smaller hotels and campgrounds cater more to those on a leisurely schedule. Some things to look for, depending on your comfort zone: hot, freshwater showers (many use salt water); bathrooms with plumbing; access to beaches; availability of taxis or other transportation; nearby restaurants; and the availability of spare hammocks hanging around for your leisure.

Hotel rates are based on double occupancy; some include meals (which are essential when there's nowhere else to eat nearby). Categories determined by price are: *Deluxe,* $250 and up *Expensive,* $90–$120 and up; *Moderate,* $60–$90; and *Inexpensive,* under $30. Prices fluctuate depending on the weather—rates are highest during the winter and spring holidays and low in late summer and fall. Some include two or three meals. Many resorts and hotels close during Sept. and Oct., when the hurricanes and rains are at their worst.

Akumal

Hotel Akumal Cancún. *Expensive.* Reservations, Avenida Bonampak y Cobá, Suites Atlantis, Local 10, Cancún, Quintana Roo, Mexico; 4 2272; in U.S, International Travel and Resorts, 800–223–9815. High-rise, hotel on the beach with 81 rooms and 11 villas just south of Club Akumal. Airconditioning, private terraces, pool, tennis court, horseback riding, game room, lounge, disco, restaurant, cable TV, dive shop, rental cars.

Hotel Aventuras Akumal. *Expensive.* Reservations, Adventure Tours, 111 Avenue Rd., Fifth Floor, Toronto M5R 3J8, 416–967–1112. Resort hotel with 44 rooms and suites and 49 condos and penthouses, swimming pool, outdoor and indoor bar, game room, dive shop, tennis, boutique, travel agency, real-estate office for condo sales.

Hotel Club Akumal Caribe and Villas Maya. *Expensive.* Reservations, Box 13326, El Paso, TX 79913; 915–584–3552 or 800–351–1622. Large sprawling resort and base for the Mexican divers organization CEDAM. Dive museum and sunken Spanish galleons. Accommodations range from thatched roof cottages to luxurious two-story condos on a long white beach. Dive shops, certification and tours, two restaurants, cocktail lounge, gift shop, tennis courts, bars, and ice-cream stand on the beach. Windsurfing, kayaks, deep-sea fishing, jungle, cenote, and cave diving.

Boca Paila

Boca Paila Fishing Lodge. *Deluxe.* Reservations, Frontiers, Box 161, Wexford, PA 15090; 800–245–1950. Bone fishing from sand flats, deep-sea fishing excursions, all meals included, and transfers to and from Cancún airport are included.

Pez Maya Fishing Resort. *Deluxe.* Reservations, World Wide Sportsmen, Box 787, Islamorada, FL 33036; 800–327–2880; in Mexico City, Melia Hotels, 905–596–2246. Bone fishing from sand flats, deep-sea fishing excursions, all meals included, and transfers to and from Cancún airport are included.

Chemuyil

Chemuyil Campground. *Inexpensive.* Pristine coconut grove on the beach with plenty of space for waterfront tent and hammock camping, or you can rent a cabana-palapa (thatch-roofed, open-air hut) with mosquito netting, hammocks and a table. The center round palapa restaurant and bar has hammocks hanging alongside the bar stools, and serves mole, tacos, and grilled fish. Small dive shop.

Chetumal

Del Prado. *Moderate.* Avenida Heroes at Chapultepec; 2 0544. The center of all that is going on in town. Air-conditioning, restaurant, and bar.

Big Ben. *Inexpensive.* Avenida Heroes #48A; 2 0965. Three-story hotel; no elevator.

Caribe Princess. *Inexpensive.* Avenida Alvaro Obregon #168; 2 0900. Small hotel, air-conditioning.

Continental Caribe. *Inexpensive.* Avenida Heroes #171; 2 1100. Refurbished old hotel with a good restaurant, bar, disco that stays open late. Air-conditioning and pool.

Crea Albergue Chetumal. *Inexpensive.* Avenida Alvaro Obregon and Paseo Veracruz; 2 3465. Government-run youth hostel, dormitories with bunk beds, pool.

El Dorado. *Inexpensive.* Avenida Cinco de Mayo #42; 2 0315. Some air-conditioned rooms, and piano bar.

Real Azteca. *Inexpensive.* Belice #186; 2 0720. Fairly new hotel near the bus station, above the Chez Farouk restaurant. Somewhat noisy, but convenient.

Ucum. *Inexpensive.* Mahatma Ghandi #167; 2 0711. Large hotel near the market with lots of guarded parking.

Felipe Carrillo Puerto

Hotel Chan Santa Cruz. *Inexpensive;* 4 0170. At the northeast end of the main plaza on Calle 68. Small hotel with courtyard.

Playa Del Carmen

Shangri-La Caribe. *Expensive.* Just north of Playa del Carmen. Turquoise Reef Group, Box 2664, Evergreen, CO 80439; 800–538–6802. Terraced bungalows with hammocks on the front porches; restaurant serving fresh fish; fruits and vegetables cleaned in purified water; bar, snorkeling, diving, windsurfing. Rate includes breakfast and dinner.

Hotel Molcas. *Expensive.* South edge of town near the ferry pier. Reservations: Aviomar, Mérida, Yucatán 99–24 6099. A 32-room hotel with large terraced pool and lounging terrace, some views of the ocean, restaurant, bar, tours.

Las Brisas Camping and Cabanas. *Inexpensive.* North of town center on beach. Rundown motel-like units with shared bathroom and shower facilities, restaurant, beach.

Posadas Lilly. *Inexpensive.* Just off Hwy. 307 on the main road into Playa del Carmen. Nondescript two-story motel, small rooms with ceiling fans and baths.

Puerto Morelos

Cabanas Playa Ojo de Agua. *Expensive.* North of town, Box 709, Mérida, Mexico; in Mérida, 21 5150. Currently being remodeled, this dive lodge books groups and individuals. Hotel rooms and cabins facing the beach, dive shop and service, freshwater pool, good restaurant for fresh fish and Yucatecan and American dishes. No telephones, no credit cards. American and European plans. Closed in Sept. and Oct.

Punta Bete

La Posada del Capitán Lafitte. *Expensive.* About 64 kms south of Cancún off Hwy. 307. Reservations in U.S., Turquoise Reef Resorts, Box 2664, Evergreen, CO 80439; 800–538–6802. 32 completely rebuilt beachfront cabanas, freshwater pool, club house, rustic oceanfront restaurant and bar, snorkeling and diving trips. Rate includes breakfast and dinner.

Kailuum. *Moderate.* About 64 km south of Cancún, on the dirt road with the Captain Lafitte sign. Reservations in U.S., Turquoise Reef Group, Box 2664, Evergreen CO 80439; 800–538–6802. A luxury campground in a coconut grove where you sleep in furnished tents or hammocks under thatched palm palapas. A large sand-floored palapa lit with candles serves as the central meeting area and dining room. Massage, beach volleyball, snorkeling, diving, windsurfing, hot showers; no electricity, no phone, no credit cards. Rate includes breakfast and dinner.

Xcalacocos. *Moderate.* At Marlin Azul sign on Hwy. 307. Tent and RV camping and 6 cabanas, showers and restrooms. Small restaurant, diving, snorkeling, and fishing gear.

Tulum

Caphe-Ha. *Deluxe.* Reservations, in Mexico City 5–254–0457; in New York 212–219–2198. An intimate hideaway that is located next to a lagoon. More of a guest house than a hotel, it's a paradise for bone fishing. Rate includes breakfast and dinner as well as transfers to and from the Cancún airport.

Cabanas Tulum. *Inexpensive.* 7 kms south of ruins on dirt road. 18 palapa bungalows with bathrooms, restaurant, bar and game room, indoor and outdoor dining, nice setting in a coconut grove.

Camping El Paraiso. *Inexpensive.* South of ruins. Cabins and camp sites; bathrooms.

Chac Mool. *Inexpensive.* South of ruins where the paved road becomes dirt. 20 palapa cabanas with beds and hammocks, camp sites, bathrooms and showers, bar; restaurant opening soon. Near Sian Ka', an underwater reserve.

Xcacel

Xcacel Camping. *Inexpensive.* Large restaurant and bar and long beach frequented by tour buses. Camping allowed on the beach; restaurant closed Sun.

DINING OUT. The restaurants along the coast are mostly simple places, specializing in the area's most abundant commodity—fish and shellfish. You'd be hard put to find an expensive spot; most are modest palapas or cafés with limited menus and low prices. Lobster, shrimp, conch, shark and a variety of fish are made into spicy marinated ceviches or grilled with butter and garlic. Yucatécan specialties such as *pollo* or *cochinita pibil, pok chuc,* and *huevos motelenos* are readily available. Bananas, coconuts, and melons are abundant and safe to eat. The restaurants at the hotels and resorts are very good, for the most part, and are great places to meet other travelers and compare notes. Price classifications are based on the average cost for dinner for one person, excluding drinks. *Expensive,* over $10; *Moderate,* $5–$10; *Inexpensive,* under $5.

Akumal

Hotel Club Akumal. *Moderate to Expensive.* The hotel has a large palapa bar-restaurant on the beach, a mid-range coffee shop type restaurant, and a gourmet restaurant on the edge of the cove, overlooking a small harbor.

Chetumal

Baalbek. *Moderate.* Avenida Heroes. Middle Eastern restaurant serving taboulleh, hummous, and pita bread.

Casablanca. *Moderate.* Madero 293; 2 3791. Good food in what might be a '40s movie set. The tavern favored by local movers and shakers.

La Cascada. *Moderate.* Hotel Continental Caribe. One of the best restaurants in town, with international cuisine.

Caribe Internacional. *Inexpensive.* On Paseo Boulevard. Lunch, snacks, drinks.

Chez Farouk. *Inexpensive.* Belice #186. Popular, somewhat noisy Middle Eastern cafe.

Los Milagros. *Inexpensive.* Zaragoza #271. Sidewalk cafe serving Yucatécan specialties.

Sergio's. *Inexpensive.* Avenida Alvaro Obregon #182. Very popular pizza parlor.

Felipe Carrillo Puerto

Restaurant 24 Horas. *Inexpensive;* 4 0020. Located on the highway just north of town, this is a good place to check out the locals and ask about a place to stay.

Playa Del Carmen

Playacar. *Moderate.* The outside deck restaurant has a great view of the beach activity and ferry pier, and has a good-sized menu with salads, sandwiches, and regional dishes.

Chac Mool. *Inexpensive.* A simple palapa on the road to the airstrip, serving fresh fish.

Puerto Morelos

Los Pelicanos and Las Palmeras. *Inexpensive.* Two small thatch-roof huts on the beach in the center of town, serving fish.

Punta Bete

Capitán Lafitte. *Moderate.* The restaurant here has two or three dinner selections each night, with the emphasis on fresh gourmet meals.

Kailuum. *Moderate.* The palapa dining area at this luxury campground was completely rebuilt after Hurricane Gilbert. The menu includes an eclectic selection of international specialties interpreted by Mayan chefs.

Tulum

El Crucero. *Inexpensive.* At the crossroads for the Tulum ruins.

El Faison y El Venado. *Inexpensive.* On the road to the ruins.

El Paraíso. *Inexpensive.* A large, pleasant, open-air palapa overlooking the ocean, serving fresh fish, cold sodas and beer, and great ceviche.

Xcaret

Restaurant Xcaret. *Inexpensive.* A small palapa on the corner of Hwy. 307 and the road to Xcaret, serving conch ceviches, lobster, *pok chuc,* and French fries. The walls are lined with photos from diving expeditions; the kitchen is open to the dining room.

HOW TO GET AROUND. Mexico Hwy. 307 runs north–south from Cancún to Chetumal, and there are few paved roads leading off toward the coast or into the jungle. The Green Angels, Mexico's guardians of the highway, patrol the road regularly and assist with breakdowns and accidents, but don't depend on them to have gas. There is a small airport in Playa del Carmen for flights to Cozumel, and Chetumal has a major international airport.

By Rental Car. Some of the resort hotels along the coast have car, Jeep and motorbike rentals for short trips in the area. The major rental companies have offices in Cancún and Cozumel (*Avis* has an office in Chetumal), but nowhere in between. Be sure to get gas whenever you can, and never let the tank run low. There is a large Pemex station in Puerto Morelos; there are Pemex stations in Playa del Carmen and Tulum, but they sometimes run out of fuel. Be sure the pump gauge is on zero before the attendant starts pumping your gas, and do your own math in figuring how much you owe. You cannot take a rental car from Mexico into Belize. Park in a guarded lot and walk across the border if you are making a day visit.

By Bus. First- and second-class buses travel the highway from early morning until dark. There is a large bus depot in the center of Playa del Carmen, and another in Chetumal, with buses to Mexico City, Villahermosa, Cancún, and Mérida.

By Taxi. No matter how small the town, there is always at least one taxi around. Fares can be ridiculously inexpensive or outrageously expensive, depending on how desperate you look and act. Always settle on the price before you take off. The distance to your destination and the type of terrain to be covered are considerations; both can certainly affect your travel time.

TOURIST INFORMATION. There is a *Government Tourist Office* in Chetumal, at Palacio del Gobierno (City Hall) (2 0266). The office is open weekdays 8 A.M.–2:30 P.M. and 6–9 P.M.

SEASONAL EVENTS. On **August** 16 in Bacalar, near Chetumal, the week-long Saint Isidro Fair is celebrated with processions, parades, cockfights, fireworks, and dances.

PARKS. *Xel-Ha,* located between Playa del Carmen and Tulum, is a national park and underwater preserve. A Mayan temple stands at the entrance to the park, just outside the row of souvenir shops and food stands that cater to the busloads of tourists from Cancún resorts. There isn't much beach at Xel-Ha; the action takes place in the water, where hordes of snorkelers float above schools of brightly colored tropical fish. Snorkeling and diving equipment can be rented from stands at the park. Landlubbers can watch the fish in a nearby lagoon, where diving is prohibited. The park's restaurant serves good ceviche, fresh fish, and drinks. The park is open from 9 A.M. until dusk. Entry fee is about 50¢.

Laguna Bacalar, 20 miles northeast of Chetumal, is often called the Lagoon of Seven Colors because of the green and blue hues that are created as salt and fresh water blend in this 50-mile-long lagoon. Water-sports concessions and restaurants are situated at the north end of the lagoon. Fort San Felipe, an 18th-century Spanish fort, is now an army post which may be toured by visitors. *Cenote Azul* on the west side of Bacalar is a 200-foot-deep well of crystal clear blue water.

MUSEUMS. A dive museum at the *Club Akumal Caribe,* off Hwy. 307 in Akumel (4–3522), has artifacts from a sunken Spanish galleon discovered just off the coast. In Chetumal, there is the *Instituto Quintanaroense de la Cultura,* at Avenida Efrain Aguilar and Andrés Quintana Roo (no phone), with art and artifacts owned by the government. The *Fuerte de*

Bacalar at Bacalar Lagoon, 20 miles from Chetumal (no phone), has a small historical museum with information on the War of Castes.

SHOPPING. There isn't much to buy along the Yucatán Coast, which relieves you of the need to rush from shop to shop during your leisure time. The road leading to the ferry in Playa del Carmen and the parking lot at the Tulum ruins are both lined with stands selling typical Mexican handicrafts, including embroidered white dresses, blouses and pants, ceramic reproductions of ruin carvings and statues, knickknacks made from shells, and some hammocks of poor quality. Even the staples of life are hard to come by—do your grocery, pharmacy, and hardware shopping in Playa del Carmen. Most of the resorts have gift shops selling post cards, film, and some handicrafts at high prices. Chetumal is a shoppers' haven for residents from other Mexican states, because of its status as a duty-free port. Items like televisions, stereos, and typewriters cost much less than they do in the rest of Mexico, but are still more expensive than in the States.

EXPLORING THE
MAYA COUNTRY

Awe-Inspiring Ruins

by
MARIBETH MELLIN

The short, dense jungles of the Yucatán Peninsula hide thousands of crumbling ruins, burying the secrets of the great Maya civilization. Temples, ball courts, nunneries, and observatories bear witness to a people of great knowledge and creativity, to a culture so intricate and unique that it defies comprehension. The mysteries of the Maya inspire curiosity and a reverential awe in the explorers who burrow ever farther into the jungle to sites as yet uncovered.

The Mayas built their city-states near Caribbean beaches and on Guatemalan plateaus. Their temples are being unearthed in the lowlands of Belize and the highlands of Chiapas. The magnificent ceremonial sites of Tikal and Palenque rise like mountainous monoliths in the impenetrable jungles. On the Yucatán Peninsula modern resorts abut ancient sacred cenotes; nowhere else are the Mayas so accessible.

The Caribbean coast's modern sun worshipers bump into the Maya past almost everywhere they turn. Hotels and parks actually have the remains of religious centers on their premises. Almost everyone signs up for an excursion to the ruins of Tulum, overlooking the jewel-toned sea. There, they become so captivated that they join more extensive tours to Cobá and Chichén Itzá.

Mérida, capital of the state of Yucatán, is regarded as the best place to get a hold on what is known of Maya history. Uxmal, Chichén Itzá, and many smaller sites are within easy driving range, and Mérida's Museum of Anthropology gives an excellent overview of the Maya regions, culture, and people.

Journey Begins at Villahermosa

Those who really want to delve into the Maya of Mexico begin their journey in Villahermosa, the capital of the state of Tabasco (the sauce named for the state is made in Louisiana). This modern city is a former hellhole, a onetime steamy river port that Graham Greene made the setting for *The Power and the Glory*. Greene would never recognize the place today. This is a boomtown made rich by oil. Pedestrian malls, luxury hotels, and an elegant shopping center are part of the scene. The only reminder of the religious persecution Greene wrote about is the singular lack of churches. That, too, is changing.

Dominating the skyline is the soaring belltower of what one day will be the Cathedral of Our Lord of Tabasco. The church, being built along colonial lines, is far from completion. One can recapture the feeling of the old days by taking a luncheon cruise aboard the *Capitán Beulo;* this converted riverboat chugs along the Grijalva into the jungle that surrounds the city, and, as it does, Greene's description of the countryside comes very much alive.

Travelers head for Villahermosa to view the Olmec sculptures in La Venta Park and the fabulous Carlos Pellicer Archaeological Museum, then head out to the imposing Maya ruins in the humid jungle at Palenque. Hardier explorers charter a flight to Bonampak, hidden deep in the jungle, and Comalcalco, one of the westernmost cities of the Maya that is still far from being excavated. Comalcalco is about 32 miles west of Villahermosa and is a curiosity for the oyster shells and clay blocks used as building materials.

The Olmecs

The Olmecs created the first advanced civilization in Mesoamerica around 1200 B.C. They disappeared about eight centuries later, leaving their mark on the civilizations just beginning to emerge. The Olmecs are sometimes called Mexico's "Mother Culture" or "The Magicians," because of this influence; many Mayan theorists believe the Olmecs were the precursors of the great Maya.

The Olmec settled in the Gulf of Mexico area, around Veracruz and Tabasco. They developed a concept of zero and a form of hieroglyphic writing which has yet to be deciphered. As a result, no one knows much about the Olmecs, the mysterious ones. All that can be said is that they developed a culture that thrived in humid, inhospitable lands, they are considered the mother culture of other civilizations that grew up in other parts of Mexico, and then, quite suddenly, they vanished.

They left their sculptures behind. Most familiar are the huge basalt heads, nine feet high and weighing 60 tons, with heavy negroid features (was there some connection with Africa?) that look for all the world like football players in old-fashioned leather helmets.

These carvings and others were found half-buried in mangrove swamps along the Gulf Coast, where there is no stone. They must have been hauled from quarries at least 60 miles away. How that was done remains a mystery. In 1957, the Olmec works were brought to Villahermosa (with great difficulty) and set up in the Parque Museo de La Venta, in tribute to the Gulf Coast site where they were originally found.

The park is an outdoor museum. The massive stone heads and other carvings are on display in a setting much like the one in which they were originally found. The highly stylized sculptures and carvings depict figures half-human, half-jaguar. The Olmecs may have believed themselves to be descended from a jaguar god; these carvings appear to represent the Rain God, the first of many deities to be worshiped in Mesoamerica. In La Venta there is also a great altar before which sits a glaring Buddha-like figure. Any Olmec communication with Asia would be unlikely, but no one can say for certain.

La Venta is one of the few places where travelers can get a real sense of the Olmecs, though the *Danzantes,* or dancers, at the ruins of Monte Albán in Oaxaca are said to be representative of Olmec art. If the Olmecs themselves were not racially the forefathers of the Mayas, culturally their influence was great. The Mayas seem to have inherited the Olmec writing, numeral, and calendar systems and the two civilizations played a similar ritualized ball game, worshiped the same rain god, and showed their piety with human sacrifices.

Evolution of Maya Civilization

The origin of the Mayas is as great an enigma as that of the Olmecs. Some students of the Maya assume that the Indians of the Americas crossed from Asia into Alaska over the Bering Strait during the Ice Age and gradually made their way south. The Mayas, some say, evolved from the Olmecs. Others say they were a totally separate civilization originating in Guatemala. They may have been late immigrants from Asia, setting up civilization beside older, more evolved immigrant cultures. In their art, some see Oriental or African influences. The Mayas represented in the ruins and living on throughout Mesoamerica appear so different from their neighbors that they seem to be an alien race. Speculation runs wild. Are they a lost tribe of Israel? Children of Atlantis? Simply another tribe? No one really can say.

What can be said is that the Mayas were the creators of one of the greatest of the ancient civilizations. Their grasp of mathematics still astounds. While the Europeans were stumbling through the Dark Ages, the Mayas were using the concept of zero and a sophisticated numerical system with complex calculations. Using a shell or similar symbol as zero, they worked out a long bar system of counting dots and dashes in units of 20. Every 20 years each settlement erected a stela, a tall column of rock with carved hieroglyphics depicting the events of the past 20-year cycle. Rulers are recognized easily; in many cases they are shown in elaborate dress, standing on the back of some poor unfortunate soul. These stelae include elaborate symbols for the gods ruling each month, and hieroglyphics telling the story of the ruler's accomplishments. Some of the most intricate stelae can still be seen at Copan, in Honduras, and at Palenque.

The Maya belief in cycles and their incredible understanding of astronomy led to an intricate time-keeping system as seen in the stelae and in carvings of the two Maya calendars. The calendars are said to be more accurate than even the 365-day Gregorian calendar we use today. The Maya Sacred Round Calendar was a 260-day religious record that fixed the dates of fiestas honoring the gods and predicted the destinies of individuals according to their birth dates. This calendar, called the *Tzolkin,* is still used in some parts of Guatemala and southern Mexico. The solar calendar, called *Haab* (a name assigned by historians and not necessarily Mayan), measures time in cycles of 52 years of a fraction more than 365 days each. Each of the 18 months consisted of 20 days. The five days left over at the end of each year were considered to be a dangerous and unlucky period called the *Uayeb.* The two calendars were meshed into a third time-keeping system, called the Calendar Round, which gave each day of the 52-year cycle a unique date. So involved were their calculations that they even predicted the universe would end when the great cycle of the long count ended on December 24, 2011. Students of the Maya have understood the calendar system since the late 1800s, but the hieroglyphics that describe events and rituals are still a puzzle gradually unwinding.

The Mayas were also advanced in technology and engineering. It is a mystery how their awe-inspiring massive ceremonial sites were built. As the excavations continue, a wide-spread highway system emerges, but the Maya did not use the wheel for transportation and had no pack animals. There was a complex chain of drainage canals and terraced planting systems. Their artistic talents are revealed in ceramics, murals, and the ornate gold and jade jewelry found in mysterious tombs and murky cenotes (deep sinkholes). The Mayas were the Greeks of the New World. J. Eric S. Thompson, a noted Maya historian, writes that if the Maya of the Classic period had held a conversation with the Classic period Greeks there would have been a mutual understanding of social systems, moral principles, religions, and cosmology. But the Maya philosophy of time is unique. They believed in the cycles of time, as ruled by the gods who determined whether those cycles would be prosperous or ominous. For the Maya, time was God.

The Mayas were farmers, raising corn, or maize. Their villages were collected in autonomous city-states, governed from great ceremonial centers. There was never a central capital ruling the entire Maya region; rather, each city-state was governed by priest-rulers who guarded their knowledge of time. Basic to the success of agriculture is knowing when to plant and when the rains will come. The secrets were learned from the stars, but learned by very few. Those who could divine the coming of the seasons were men of magic, magicians who became priests. Priests ruled, for the most powerful man holds the secret of his people's survival.

Only a man who controlled arms might challenge a priest. Once a village had a bulging granary, it was a tempting target for raiders. Defenders needed to be recruited and trained. Defensive troops can easily become an offensive army. A village may survive on what it grows, but it becomes rich by looting from others. Warrior chiefs who led the looting became kings. For a long time, students of the Maya held a romantic notion that the Maya were a peace-loving, gentle civilization, unlike their warfaring neighbors. But archaeologists continue to uncover data that reveal a series of wars between states, and a religious belief in human sacrifice and mutilation. The Maya traditionally used a wooden brace to deform the heads of their children to produce an oval shape, and ritualistically pierced their tongues, earlobes, and genitals, offering their blood to the gods.

The great Maya cities now in ruins, archaeologists say, were not so much inhabited places as ceremonial centers. They grew in splendor as princes and priests sought to outdo each other. Over the centuries, temples arose atop pyramids. Builders burrowed through subterranean layers of previous buildings, erecting burial tombs in the deepest centers of ancient temples. Atop the latest edifice, great palaces were built. It seems only the highest of the ruling classes lived in these ceremonial centers; the peasants huddled in huts much like those still seen in Maya villages. Naturally, it was the peasants who built these massive monuments. Did they ever rebel? Were the periodic declines and falls of Maya cities the result of peasant uprisings? Or did proud kings slaughter arrogant priests only to find that with them they had killed the secrets of when to sow? The stories may be told in the glyphs carved on walls and on the stelae at many sites. Of late some progress has been made in deciphering them.

Though the Maya were spread over much of Mesoamerica, different regions prospered at different times. The Maya civilization has been divided into three approximate periods when major developments took place. Though the dates change as archaeologists and anthropologists unravel each mystery, the periods are usually classified as the Pre-Classic era, beginning around 1700 B.C.; the Classic period, from A.D. 300 to 900; and the Post-Classic period, from A.D. 900 to 1530. The Maya civilization disintegrated after A.D. 900. By the time the Spaniards arrived in the 1500s, little evidence remained of the glory and grandeur of this highly evolved civilization. Again, no one really knows why.

Arrival of Spaniards

When the Spaniards arrived, their earliest expeditions were driven from the shores by fierce native warriors. Then in 1527, nearly a decade after Cortés had conquered the Aztecs, Francisco de Montejo won royal permission to subdue Yucatán. He met with no quick success. Routed from what is now the coast of Quintana Roo, Montejo decided he was too old for the conquest business and turned it over to his son. Montejo junior opted to attack the peninsula's other shore. It was he who settled Campeche and from there moved south. Some 20 years were required for the Montejos to establish Spanish rule on the Yucatán Peninsula. Victory was won not so much by arms as disease. Smallpox and measles decimated the Mayas.

Many of those who survived retreated inland. Only the eastern coast of the region really came under Spanish domination. The great battles were still to come as missionaries waged what has come to be called the spiritual conquest, and here the casualties in some respects were the highest of all. Every Mayan book that could be found was destroyed. The zeal of the church in destroying what is considered works of the devil is completely understandable considering attitudes at that time, but the loss to humanity was enormous. Fray Diego de Landa, the third Bishop of Yucatán, is simultaneously credited with destroying and recording the history of the Mayas. While stationed in Mani, Landa systematically destroyed cultural artifacts, burned all written records and codices and castigated those Indians who tried to remain true to their traditions. At the same time, he compiled a wealth of information on the Maya from which he wrote his treatise, called *Relación de las cosas Yucatán* (Report on the things of Yucatán). Today, Landa's report is a most important record of the Maya culture and traditions as they existed in the 1500s. But Landa's destruction was equally thorough. Only three original Maya codices remain, and they are housed in museums in Dresden, Paris, and Madrid.

The religion of the Mayas never was entirely stamped out. Often it blended with Christianity, the gods of the ancients taking on the names of the saints. Mass became another ritual. The Maya civilization had been in decline for 500 years before the Europeans came. It continued to decline in bush villages, but never did it disappear.

On the coast Spain ruled for 300 years. Pirates were the worst worry, especially in Campeche, but they never threatened the system. What brought that down was Mexican independence. Yucatán was then a separate jurisdiction, ruled directly by the Spanish crown. But when the viceroy of New Spain yielded to the mainland freedom fighters, the governor of Yucatán resigned as well. After some debate, and in return for considerable autonomy, Yucatán chose to throw in its lot with Mexico and with some reservations joined the new federation.

It was an attempt to impose a strong central government in Mexico that led Texas to break away from Mexico in 1836. Four years later Yucatán followed its example. Like Texas, Yucatán sought to join the U.S. Washington declined the offer, but Yucatán refused to make its peace with Mexico City. In an effort to defend independence the peninsula's rulers—great landholders descended from Spanish conquerors—chose to arm the Mayas.

War of the Castes

Arming the Mayas, from the landholders' point of view, turned out to be a dreadful mistake. It touched off a civil struggle that lasted for generations. This was the War of the Castes.

Under Spanish rule the people of the colonies were classified according to birth. At the top were the Peninsulars, the natives of Spain, who ruled. Then there were the Creoles, offspring of Peninsulars born in the colony. Beneath them were the Indians and those of mixed blood; every combination had a name. These were the *castas,* the castes. In the 1840s the Indians, the castes, were given arms to defend the Creoles. Instead, they rose up against them.

What began as a rebellion grew into a movement to reestablish a kingdom of the Mayas. Yucatán's Creoles quickly terminated their own secessionist movement, rejoining the Mexican federation with Campeche as a separate state. Troops came in from the mainland, but the Mayas, while they retreated, never surrendered.

Chan Santa Cruz ("Little Holy Cross" in Maya Spanish) in what is now Quintana Roo became the Maya capital. Here a small wooden cross is said to have spoken to the Maya rebels, urging them to fight on. Fight they did—and for more than half a century. The Mexican Revolution, the great social upheaval that broke out in 1910, finally brought an end to the fighting. Federal troops, being occupied elsewhere, simply withdrew. The Mayas were left running their own affairs.

The more enlightened rulers brought in by the revolution reached something of an informal compromise. The lands ruled by the Mayas were broken off from the state of Yucatán and made a federal territory, Quintana Roo (named, somewhat ironically, for Andrés Quintana Roo, a nineteenth-century figure who had been instrumental in convincing Yucatán to join the Mexican Union). Chan Santa Cruz became Felipe Carrillo Puerto in honor of a Revolutionary governor of Yucatán who was deposed and shot by his enemies. After that the Mayas were pretty much left to their own devices. As the decades passed, younger Mayas began pressing not to be left so much alone. The benefits of development were wanted and jobs were needed. Thus Cancún was built, and in 1974 Quintana Roo became a state. But in much of Quintana Roo the Maya people live as their ancestors did.

The Modern Maya

The Maya of today live much like the peasants in the Classic era. Small villages and towns dot the Yucatán peninsula with clusters of traditional Maya homes. These huts are normally oval-shaped, with logs or reeds laced together upright to form the walls, and palm fronds laid over a peaked wooden frame for the roof. Homes are grouped according to familial units, near the family's farmland. The traditional Maya hut has a central room with a dirt floor and hammocks hanging in the sleeping area. Hennequen bags hanging from the walls hold the family's possessions; a fire ring surrounded by *canchés,* small wooden benches, sits in the center. Today, metal cookware and plastic dishes sit beside traditional clay water jugs and gourd utensils, and couches and beds are replacing the hammocks.

The Maya have melded their ancient religious rituals with the Christianity enforced upon them by the Spaniards. Ceremonies honoring the rain god (*Chac*) take place in the fields of corn and hennequen. Other rituals to *Itzamna,* Lord of the Heavens, *Ah Kin,* the sun god, and *Yum Kax,* the corn god, are still performed on their own or are combined with saints' days and celebrated in the churches. This combination of religions and philosophies seems like an anachronism, an awkward blend of paganism and Christianity. But the Mayas are not confused; they simply substituted saints for their gods, but continued thinking of them as gods ruling the elements and protecting the animals and people. Every little Mayan hamlet has its annual fiesta honoring the town's patron saint; at these times, the blend of religions becomes most apparent.

As with many other Indian groups, the Mayas are also replacing their traditional style of dress. Many women still wear the *huipil* embroidered dress over long white slips, but the men have largely abandoned their loose, high-collared white shirts and gathered pants for polyester slacks and *guyaberas.* The women still carry their children and goods in lightweight *rebozos* or shawls wound intricately around their shoulders and heads.

Though cars are common and the main highways run through many Maya villages, the people in these small towns rely primarily on bicycles for transportation. It is not uncommon to see an entire family riding along on one bike frame, the father pedaling along as the mother sits on the seat and the children hang from all ends.

Maya languages continue to flourish on the peninsula, though many people now speak a combination of Maya and Spanish. Most Mayas on the peninsula speak Yucatec, though there are many Maya tongues, some still used in other regions. The Lancandón, who number only 300 or so, still inhabit remote regions of Chiapas, around Bonampak and Palenque, and are perhaps the most authentic, traditional Maya left in Mesoamerica. Yet even they have become accustomed to the sight of Western scholars and travelers, and are slowly adapting more to modern civilization.

Prominent Maya Sites Outside Yucatán

At the peak of the Classic period, Maya territory extended over 117,000 square miles throughout Mesoamerica. The remote sites in the highlands and lowlands of Chiapas, Guatemala, Honduras, and Belize are visited mostly by devoted amateur and expert Maya buffs. In these regions only Tikal, a magnificent center in the jungle of Guatemala, is a common tourist stop. The majority of travelers interested in the Maya begin their explorations in Palenque, about 90 miles southeast of Villahermosa.

The drive to Palenque passes through thick, steaming jungle to a center well worth the inconvenience of travel. The landscape here is a deep, tropical green with a small stream running through the jungle so dense it threatens to overtake the ruins once again. The most significant buildings are the Temple of Inscriptions, with its recently uncovered burial tomb and wondrous view of the city, and Temples XII and XIII, first visible from the path into the jungle. Palenque flourished in the Classic period, reaching its peak about A.D. 600. It was abandoned around A.D. 900.

Most visitors to Palenque head out from Villahermosa early in the day and return about dusk. For those who want to see more— Palenque, surrounded by jungle hills, is most impressive early in the day—there is a choice of several decent hotels.

Bonampak, one of the most famous Maya sites and also one of the most inaccessible, can be reached by air taxi or Jeep from Palenque. A small site surrounded by jungle, Bonampak is noted for murals that really bring the Maya past to life. The Lancandón Indians kept the temple in Bonampak and its vivid paintings a secret for centuries; the site was discovered by an American expatriate in 1946. Many feel that Bonampak is not worth the expensive trip. One should know about Bonampak, but the fact is that reproductions of the murals—the best are in Mexico City's Museum of Anthropology—are better than the real thing. Efforts to enhance the real murals at Bonampak have only faded them further. The site itself is small but not at all unimpressive.

Very much worthwhile, on the other hand, is pushing on from Palenque into the Chiapas highlands. It will take the better part of a day to get to San Cristobal de las Casas—the trip is spectacularly beautiful—and a couple of more days will be needed just to wander around before backtracking to Villahermosa. This is the home of the Highland Maya, people who even more than their cousins in Yucatán maintain their customs, traditions, and ancient way of life.

The Maya explorer will push on from Villahermosa to Campeche, the capital of the state of Campeche. The ruins of the Maya center at Edzna are about an hour's drive from Campeche. Of late Edzna has been attracting attention as possibly the place where the Maya calendar—actually more accurate than the one the world uses today—may have been devised. The fact that the sun reaches its zenith over Edzna on what would be the Mayas' New Year's Day has led to this theory. In other respects, the ruins, largely undisturbed since they were discovered, will impress only archaeology buffs.

The Maya of the Yucatán Peninsula

Mérida, the capital of the state of Yucatán, was built on the ruins of the Maya City of *T'Hó* in 1542. It is a natural center from which to study the Maya, starting with the Archaeological Museum's excellent exhibits of the evolution of this impressive civilization. On the city streets, one sees the Maya of today, a genial, gentle people with a distinctive look. Everything in Mayaland, as fans tend to call the region, is short—the people, the jungles, the homes, and city buildings. In comparison to the big cities in central Mexico, Mérida and Mayaland are pristinely clean. The humidity, heat, persistent mosquitos, and torrential rainstorms don't seem to affect the Mayas in the least; they seem imperturbed about almost everything. Many of the people in the city wear modern clothing and speak flawless Spanish and some English, but there is little masking of their heritage. The shops and neighborhoods have decidely Mayan names, with plenty of Ks and Zs to give conversation a Mayan sound. The Mayas are a people with only partial interest in assimilation. Through onslaughts from the warring city-states, the Toltecs, Spaniards, pirates, and Mexican army, the Maya have retained much of their ancient culture.

From Mérida one can travel north on Highway 261 to Progreso's gulf beaches and stop at *Dzibilchaltún* (Mayan for "where there is writing on rocks"), one of the earliest Pre-Classic settlements. A small museum records the site's history from 1000 B.C. to the Spanish invasion in the sixteenth century. The sacred cenote is one of the deepest on the peninsula; divers have recovered thousands of artifacts and human bones, suggesting the well was used for sacrifices to the gods. The Temple of the Seven Dolls is of interest because of the seven male dolls found deep in the temple, beneath newer structures. The dolls were deformed and made of vulcanized rubber, virtually unknown in the region, though recent explorers have found that the Lacandón Indians in Chiapas make similar dolls. A Spanish chapel built with rocks from the ruins in 1590 sits to one side, evidence of the Spaniard's attempt to overcome this long-lasting Maya ceremonial center.

The southwest route from Mérida on Highways 180 and 261 passes Maya villages, ruin sites, and an extensive cenote zone on the route to Uxmal, a spectacular ceremonial center.

Oft-Built Uxmal

Uxmal, hidden in the rolling green hills of the Puuc range, is easily one of the most impressive of all Maya sites. The steep pyramids are built into natural hills, rising from rocky ridges. It is easy to visit Uxmal in a day's trip from Mérida, but much more rewarding to spend the night in a pleasant hotel, see the light-and-sound show at the ruins at night, and drive the 80-mile loop southwest of Uxmal with its series of sites on the way back to Mérida the next day.

Uxmal, tour guides will tell you, means "Thrice Built." They will then add Uxmal was rebuilt at least five times. The center first flourished sometime in the 7th century, about the era when Palenque was reaching its peak. It was abandoned and reoccupied on a few occasions, and was built in several stages during the Late Classical period, then abandoned again. No one can say with any certainty why. The invading Toltecs in the 10th century seized what may well have been little more than a ghost town, held on there for awhile and then evacuated. Finally Uxmal became a rather pure Maya ceremonial center of the Post Classic era. It was deserted for the last time some 90 years before the Spanish conquest began.

The architecture is what sets Uxmal apart. Lines are clean and uncluttered and the buildings themselves in excellent repair. It would seem that the successive waves of groups that made Uxmal theirs chose to honor the designs. In some cases efforts were made to improve upon them, but seldom were they radically changed.

Worshiped here with great fervor was Chac, the elephant-snouted rain god whose face appears throughout Yucatán. The people of Uxmal had good reason to be reverent toward him, for water in these parts is scarce. There are no cenotes or sink-holes. The Mayas dug cisterns, called *chultunes,* for collecting rainwater when it came. Drought may be the reason Uxmal was abandoned so often. The theme of the light-and-sound show centers upon the dependence of the people on rain.

Really the best thing about this spectacle is the way the artificial light brings out details of carvings and mosaics so easy to miss when the sun is shining. There are, for example, replicas of Maya huts reproduced in stone on one facade in the quadrangle. They resemble almost identically the huts still to be seen in many Maya villages today. The light-and-sound show is shown nightly in Spanish and English. It is said to be one of the best of such shows. Travel agencies from Mérida offer afternoon and evening tours to Uxmal with dinner at a nearby restaurant before the show. At night, Uxmal has a sense of mystery. And by moonglow the unique rounded Pyramid of the Magician, said to have been built overnight by a magical dwarf, takes on added beauty.

The Pyramid of the Magician faces west, toward the sun, has an unusual oval shape, and stands about 100 feet high. The western stairway slopes at a 60-degree angle—once you reach the top, the view of the city of Uxmal and the surrounding hillsides is impressive. The Nunnery (named by the Spaniards) is a group of four buildings, decorated with latticework, masks, geometric patterns, and animal carvings; one wall is covered with red hand prints. The Palace of the Governor is considered by some to be the finest example of pre-Hispanic art in Mesoamerica. Its 320-foot length is separated by three corbeled arches, creating narrow passageways or sanctuaries. The friezes along the uppermost section of the palace are as intricate as any in Mayaland, with carvings of geometric patterns overlaid with plumed serpents and Chac masks. These mosaics are said to have required over 20,000 individually cut stones.

Staying at an Uxmal hotel allows one ample time to really explore Uxmal, particularly in the early morning and evening when it can seem as though you are all alone with the magnificence of the Maya of old. It also allows time to visit the other Maya ruins in the area along a newly paved road cutting from Sayil, off Highway 261, to Oxkutzcab on Highway 184. Kabah, about 14 miles south of Uxmal on Highway 261, is rather fascinating because of its Temple of the Masks (also called the Codz Poop) with an entire facade covered by 300 hook-nosed images of Chac. The freestanding Arch of Kabah is one of the finest of the Maya arches; it marks the end of an ancient limestone-topped road (now overgrown) leading to Uxmal.

Sayil is nearly buried by dirt and thorny bushes, the sides of its three-story palace covered with rubble. A few other buildings are scattered through the overgrown site. A Maya family lives in a traditional hut on the grounds and sells sodas, snacks, souvenirs, and a nice selection of books on the Mayas. Labná's ceremonial arch is much more ornate than the one at Kabah. Its palace was never finished, but is still an unusual building, with second-story apartments and a large mask of Chac.

The Caves of Loltún, five miles south of Oxkutzcab, contain an underground system of enormous caverns and passageways with Mayan sculptures and surrealistic shapes formed by stalactites. The name Loltún means "Flower of the Rock," possibly referring to the the petal-shaped rooms off one passageway.

The contemporary Maya town of Mani, at the northeast point of the Maya-route loop, is infamous as the site where Fray Diego de Landa, a Spanish Franciscan zealot, burned nearly all the

Mayan books and documents. A huge 16th-century church and monastery stands in the center of town, and was built in a short seven months with the labor of the Mayas, who were beaten for honoring their Mayan gods. Mani also has the cenote where the wicked mother of the magical dwarf who built the Uxmal pyramid is said to live. Legend has it that the mother would make the well run dry and demanded babies to be tossed in as a sacrifice to get the water flowing again.

Mayapán, north of Mani on Yucatán Highway 18, was the last of the great Maya cities, founded in the 11th century at the end of the Post Classic period. Some 3,500 buildings have been discovered in this enormous archaeological zone. The temples and altars are insignificant when compared with those at Uxmal and Chichén Itzá, and the site is far from developed.

Ticul, a Mayan town at the Intersection of the ruins road and Highway 184, is an excellent place to stop for lunch. Its main restaurant, *Los Almendros,* has a reputation for serving the best Yucatán regional cuisine to be found anywhere, and the prices are exceptionally low. The outdoor patio is pleasant when there's a breeze in the air. The Ticul restaurant recently celebrated its twenty-sixth anniversary; a newer branch is quite popular in Mérida. Ticul is the pottery center of Yucatán, and the streets are lined with yards full of red clay pots for sale.

Chichén Itzá

Chichén Itzá is about 75 miles east of Mérida on Highway 180 east toward the Caribbean resorts. A more leisurely and scenic route is to take Highway 80 west from Mérida and pass through Tixkokob, a Maya community famous for its hammock weavers. By cutting south at Tekanto and east again at Citilcúm (the road has no number and there are a precious few road signs), one reaches Izamal. This city is interesting for its uniformity—every building is painted an earth-toned yellow that gives the city the nickname *Ciudad Amarilla* ("Yellow City"). A huge sixteenth-century Franciscan monastery sits atop a sacred cenote in the center of town. The dogged Bishop de Landa supervised the completion of the monastery, begun by Fray Juan de Merida in 1553 to supplant the heathen temple which once stood there. The church, with its rows of yellow arches and gigantic atrium, is one of the largest religious structures in Mexico. A few blocks northeast of the main plaza is a partially excavated Maya site atop a high hill. The pyramid, called Kinich Kakmo, is difficult to climb because of the crumbling steps, but has a wonderful view of the surrounding countryside— flat fields of maguey cactus broken only by an occasional clump of trees. On clear days it is possible to spot Chichén Itzá, some 30 miles southeast.

A one- or two-night stop at Chichén Itzá is highly recommended. The town of Pisté, about a mile west of the ruins has a few hotels, motels and campgrounds. The hotels by the ruin site are delightful, restful resorts, and the archaeological zone is the most extensively restored and, in some respects, the most extraordinary of the pre-Hispanic centers.

Highway 180 bypasses the ruin site, but the old road divides Chichén Itzá chronologically. Old Chichén, on the south side of the road, is representative of the Classic period, with buildings constructed around A.M. 600. New Chichén, on the north side of the road, reflects the period after the Toltecs conquered the Maya in the 10th century.

Chichén Itzá is known best as a Maya–Toltec center. The Toltec invaders from the mainland made this their religious captial, and the ruins are a monument both to their warlike ways and to the genius of the Mayas. Nowhere is this better seen than at the pyramid called *El Castillo* (The Castle) that dominates the site and is visible above all the other buildings.

El Castillo is topped by a temple to Kukulkán (known as Quetzacoatl in mainland Mexico), the deity represented by a feathered snake that led the Toltecs on their migration to Yucatán. A climb of 91 steps reaches the top temple; those fearful of heights can hold on to a rusted chain running down the center of the steps. El Castillo is fraught with symbolism, with the four stairways facing the cardinal directions, the steps totaling 365, representing the days of the year. Fifty-two panels on the sides stand for the 52 years of the Mayan calendar; the 18 terraces represent the 18 months of the religious year. By the base of one balustrade is carved a great serpent head. At the spring and fall equinox, March 21 and September 21, the afternoon lights and shadows strike the balustrade in such a way to form a shadow picture representing Kukulkan undulating out of his temple and wriggling down the pyramid to bless the fertile earth. The engineering skill that went into this amazing project boggles the mind. Thousands of people travel to Chichén to witness this sight, particularly in the spring since there is always the chance that the fall rains will spoil the spectacle. It is advisable to make hotel reservations well in advance—a year ahead is not unreasonable.

Archaeologists have discovered a more ancient temple inside the Castillo, where a slippery wet stairway leads upward to an altar holding two statues—a Chac Mool and a bejeweled red tiger. Upon discovery, the tiger wore a mosaic disc of jade and turquoise, now in the National Anthropology Museum in Mexico City. The inner temple is open to the public during only a few hours in the morning and again for a few hours in the afternoon. Those prone to claustrophobia should take heed—the stairs are narrow, dark, and winding, and most days there is a line of tourists going both ways, making the trip somewhat frightening.

Nearby is a ball court, similar to those found at other ancient centers in Mexico but bigger and more elaborate. The game played was something like soccer (no hands were to be used) and it fascinated the Europeans; indeed it might be said that one of Mexico's gifts to the Old World was team sports and rubber balls. To the Mayas and their neighbors ballgames apparently had religious significance. A carving at the court shows what appears to be a player being sacrificed by decapitation, blood spurting from his severed neck to fertilize the earth. The acoustics are so great that a person standing at one end of the 140-yard court can clearly hear the whispers of another person standing at the other end.

More sacrifices took place at the Sacred Well, a cenote about a half mile from the main ceremonial area. Once it was believed that virgins were hurled into these waters to appease the rain gods, but diving archaeologists have since discovered skeletons belonging to individuals of all ages. The story goes that men, women, and children were all thrown into the well to appease the gods in the early morning. The slippery walls were impossible to climb, and most could not swim well enough to survive until noon, when those who did hang on were fished out to relate the stories of what they had learned from the spirits in the water. Thousands of artifacts of gold and jade, items highly precious to the Mayas, have also been found in the murky depths of the cenote, which undoubtedly holds more treasures. Trees and shrubs have been washed into the well over the centuries, and their remains have prevented divers from getting to the bottom. Since the pool is fed by a network of underground rivers, it cannot be drained.

New Chichén is enormous—it can take days to explore fully the many buildings, most significant of which are the Group of the Thousand Columns, and the temples of the Warriors, Jaguars, and the Bearded Man. Old Chichén is equally intriguing to the Mayan enthusiast, with its ancient buildings over-grown by flowering vines. El Caracol (the snail) is a famous Mayan astronomical observatory, built in several stages with additions of skull-shaped incense burners from the Toltecs. The Nunnery (named by the Spaniards) has long intricately carved panels. Maya guides will willingly lead you down the path by an old narrow-guage railroad track to even more ruins, barely unearthed.

Chichén Itzá has much to see and explore. The light-and-sound show in the evening is not as well done as the one at Uxmal, but it provides a form of after-dark entertainment as the colored lights enhance the carvings on El Castillo's walls. The archaeological zone is open from 8 A.M. to 5 P.M., and is guarded at night. The entrance fee is about 50 cents. There are no restaurants at the site, but there are soda, fruit, snack, and souvenir stands in the parking lot.

Just a couple of miles from Chichén Itzá is the Cave of Balancanchén, a Maya shrine discovered in 1959. It was virtually undisturbed since the time of the conquest. Within it is the largest collection of artifacts yet found in Yucatán, mostly vases and jars once filled with offerings. An image of the rain god rises about a small underground lake in which blind fish swim. Guided tours, which depart on the hour (noon and 1 P.M. are skipped; the last tour leaves at 4 P.M.), are mandatory for visitors to the cave. Even then one must be in fairly good physical shape, for considerable crawling is required. Claustrophobics should avoid Balancanchén.

The town of Pisté serves mostly as a base camp for travelers to Chichén Itzá. The hotels, restaurants, and handicraft shops are normally more expensive than elsewhere. There is a Pemex station at the west end of town and a bank that will not exchange travelers checks for pesos.

From Chichén Itzá east toward the Caribbean, the highway winds through Valladolid. Second-largest city in the state of Yucatán, Valladolid is picturesque, pleasant, and provincial. It has a couple of inexpensive hotels and passable places to eat. A turnoff here leads north to Rio Lagartos (Alligator River). Flamingos in grand flocks make this neighborhood home. Seeing these long-necked pink birds soaring above the water and watching them settle in great red clouds makes the detour worthwhile. Rio Lagartos, with its palmy beaches, supposedly one day will be developed into a seaside resort. Yucatán authorities have been talking about that for years. More likely it will be promoted among sportsmen. Tarpon fishing and hunting for deer and boar are excellent here.

From Rio Lagartos motorists can either take a shortcut back to Mérida or return to Valladolid and head east into Quintana Roo. Cancún and the Mexican Caribbean are no more than two hours away.

Cobá

A trip to Cobá, with the possibility of spending the night there, has much to recommend it. The towering pyramids, soaring above the rain forest, are the most majestic in Mexico. The setting of what was once a great city on the shores of five lakes is ghostly in its beauty.

Not long ago, one had to drive east to Cancún, then south to Tulum in order to reach the road running west again to Cobá. Now there are two paved roads running from Highway 180 to the ruins, one at Chemex 30 miles east of Vallodalid, and another at Nuevo X-Can, just inside the Quintana Roo border. (The road from Chemex begins as an unpaved road and is hard to find.) The condition of both roads is unpredictable. Road signs constantly warn drivers to reduce their speed; the straight road is mesmerizing and wild animals running across the pavement can cause dreadful accidents. There are no gas stations or settlements of any type along this road; be sure to check your gas, water and oil before heading through the jungle to Cobá.

Cobá was inhabited by about 400 B.C., but it seems to have got its start as a true city about A.D. 600. The Spaniards never discovered Cobá; thus the ruins are in better shape than those that were destroyed to make way for Christianity. The remains of 30 wide roads—they must have been more impressive than today's highways, although they were used only by human bearers since the Mayas had no beasts of burden—indicate this was a great center of commerce. There was considerable trade, apparently, with the Mayas of Tikal in what is now Guatemala.

Cobá is an enormous archaeological zone with clusters of ceremonial centers built on the shores of five lakes. It behooves the traveler to carry a map of the ruins, a canteen, and a heavy dose of bug repellent. The jungle paths running through this zone that once held 40,000 inhabitants are confusing at best.

A 1½-mile walk through the sweltering jungle leads to the tallest pyramid at Cobá. Nohuch-Mul towers 140 feet over the jungle and contains at its top a temple honoring that mysterious figure found at Tulum, the Descending God. The climb up the 140 steps is a difficult one. There is another pyramid nearby, this one with a now empty tomb. All about are remnants of temples. About 30 carved stelae have been found at Cobá, some with intricate hieroglyphs depicting the history of Cobá. They show some rather tyrannical rulers, lords—and, in one case, a lady—standing imperiously on the backs of either captives, subjects, or slaves.

Cobá is quite extensive. Two or three miles separate one group of ruins from the next. Excavation of the site began in 1973, and seven groups of dwellings and temples have been uncovered. It is estimated that there are some 6,500 structures in the area, evidence that this was one of the greatest Mayan city-states.

One must have a car to visit Cobá; there is a bus that runs from Tulum, 30 miles east on the coast, to Cobá, but it is not reliable. Some small restaurants and shops are clustered at the entrance to the ruins, and there is a small entrance fee. The only recommendable hotel in the area is the Villa Archeologica.

Tulum

Tulum, about 80 miles south of Cancún, is one of the most beautiful and fascinating of the many ancient Maya sites found on the Yucatán Peninsula. It is truly unique. This was the only Maya city built right on the coast, the only one protected by a wall, and the only one known to have been inhabited when the conquistadors arrived.

Although archaeologists have found indications Tulum was settled 1,500 years ago, most of the present buildings are no more than 800 years old. They belong to the late Post-Classic period when the Maya civilization was in its decline. Certain artistic refinements found elsewhere are missing here, but the excellent state of preservation more than makes up for that. And the castle, *El Castillo*, that dominates the area, is impressive. The castle has now been identified as a temple to Kukulkán, the feathered snake deity introduced by the Toltecs, the Indian horde that swept in from central

Mexico and conquered the Mayas only to be absorbed by them. The Toltecs have vanished; the Mayas live on.

Believers in unidentified flying objects and others convinced that the earth once was visited by tiny aliens from some other planet have made Tulum a shrine of their own. They hold in greatest reverence the Temple of the Descending God. Over the doorway is a carved figure that does indeed appear to be tumbling from the heavens. More prosaic scholars claim this represents either the setting sun or a bee (the Mayas were and are great producers of honey).

Still it is a fact that Maya myth maintains Tulum was first built by prodigious dwarfs. Many of the lesser temples are indeed tiny. Entranceways do seem designed to accommodate little people. Archaeologists, however, insist low doorways were so designed that those who entered would be forced to bow if not crawl, this being only proper when approaching a god.

Tulum in its final days is believed to have been a seaside trading center. It may have been a haven for the Chontal, a Maya group from the Campeche side of the peninsula who operated a merchant fleet of canoes that made regular trips to Central America. Or Tulum may have been a satellite of Cobá, once a city of 50,000 about 25 miles inland.

Kohunlich

A relatively recently discovered Mayan site 35 miles east of Chetumal Kohunlich, is the last stop on your tour of significant Maya sites on the Yucatán Peninsula. The Pyramid of the Masks is particularly interesting for its portrayals of the Sun God, the largest of which is a carving ten feet tall. The ten-square-mile site is still under excavation, and it is estimated that there are some 200 buildings in the area, though only five have been uncovered.

PRACTICAL INFORMATION FOR

THE MAYA COUNTRY

CHICHÉN ITZÁ

HOW TO GET THERE. It is easiest to reach and explore Chichén Itzá by **car.** First- and second-class **buses** travel the route between Mérida and Cancún regularly, with stops in Piste and Valladolid. There is a small airstrip just off Hwy. 180 where private planes from Mérida, Cozumel and Cancún regularly transport travelers.

ACCOMMODATIONS. The hotels serving Chichén Itzá are located primarily in Pisté, about one mile from the ruins. The more elegant resorts are on the dirt road running between the south entrance to the ruins and

Hwy. 180. The south entrance to the ruins is within easy walking distance from these hotels, which makes it easy to climb about in the morning, relax by the pool in the afternoon, and visit the ruins again before they close as the sun sets. The surroundings are decidedly reminiscent of tropical jungles, with a cacaphony of bird songs from the blooming jacarandas in the early morning. It's best to make reservations while in Mérida, Cancún, or Cozumel. The price categories listed here are for double rooms without meals: *Expensive,* $45 and up; *Moderate,* $30–$45; *Inexpensive,* under $30. Expensive hotels accept most credit cards; many of the others do not.

Expensive

Hotel Hacienda Chichén. Just a short walk from the ruins, 6 2777. This historic 17th-century hacienda has seen better days, and resembles an enchanted (or haunted) mansion. An old, enormous swimming pool sits in the middle of the landscaped gardens. The dining room and bar are in the main mansions. The Hacienda is closed from late spring until mid-Nov. For reservations, write Box 407, Mérida, Yucatán, Mexico.

Hotel Mayaland. On the dirt road ¼ mile south of ruins; 6 2777. An enchanting resort hotel with small Mayan cottages tucked along beautifully landscaped pathways nearly overgrown with blooming bougainvillea and huge mangrove trees. The rooms in the central building have terraces overlooking fountains, statues, and tropical flower gardens. The alcoves on the road side of the hotel have a beautiful view of El Caracol at Old Chichén. Ceiling fans keep the rooms cool while mosquito nets and screens keep the bugs out. The restaurant and bar are expensive, but charming, and there is a large swimming pool. For reservations, write to same address as Hotel Hacienda Chichén Itzá.

Hotel Misión Chichén Itzá. In Pisté, 1½ miles west of the ruins; in U.S., 800–431–2138. An attractive two-story hotel with 40 rooms around a central garden with adult and children's swimming pools. Tiled rooms, air-conditioning, restaurant, bar, poolside bar, dining terrace. Rate includes breakfast and lunch or dinner.

Villa Archeologica. On the dirt road ½ mile south of the ruins; 4 4915 or in the U.S., 800–258–2633. A Club Med resort at the ruins, this hotel is newer than Mayaland but still charming in its own way. The restaurant has an extensive gourmet menu. Tennis courts, swimming pool, air-conditioned rooms with Mediterranean decor and handmade tiles in the bathrooms.

Moderate

Piramide Inn. In Pisté, 1½ miles west of ruins. Roadside hotel, large air-conditioned rooms, swimming pool, gardens, dining room. For reservations, write Box 433, Mérida, Yucatán, Mexico.

Inexpensive

Hotel Dolores Alba. 1½ miles east of ruins on Hwy. 180; 21 3745, in Mérida. This small hotel is run by the family that owns the Dolores Alba in Mérida. Some air-conditioned rooms, a pretty terrace by a small pool, small dining area with personal service. The owners will drive you to the ruins, and the buses traveling on the highway will stop if you wave them down.

Piramide Inn Trailer Park. Beside the Piramide Inn Hotel. Electrical and water hookups for RVs, use of the pool at the hotel. For reservations, write Piramide Inn, above.

DINING OUT. Pisté is not a gourmand's town. The fare in most of the restaurants is simple, over-priced, and only fair. The hotel restaurants are your best bets; most of the restaurants in town are obviously set up to handle large tour-bus crowds and are empty the rest of the time. Prices for an average dinner for one without drinks are: *Expensive,* over $10; *Moderate,* $5–$10; *Inexpensive,* under $5. None of the restaurants have phones, so reservations are obviously unnecessary.

The only restaurants in the *Expensive* category are those at the **Hotel Mayaland, Villa Archeologica,** and **Hacienda Chichén.** Of these, the one at Villa Archeologica is, in culinary terms, the best.

Fiesta Restaurant. *Moderate.* About 2 miles from the ruins in Pisté. A large restaurant with Formica tables in front and a large group room in the back with murals covering the walls. Yucatécan dishes, good breakfasts.

Restaurant Xaybe. *Moderate.* About 1 mile from the ruins in Pisté. This enormous, immaculately clean restaurant caters to tour-bus groups, but even when none are around, the tables are set with cloth napkins and wine glasses. Yucatecan specialties and beef dishes.

Inexpensive meals are hard to come by in Pisté, though there are quite a few small palapa-type cafés along the main road. Check the menu prices before you order. There are a few small markets and produce stands where you can gather a picnic lunch of fruit and bread.

HOW TO GET AROUND. Hwy. 180 passes straight through Pisté, then curves south at the main entrance to the ruins. About 2 miles past the main entrance there are hotel and ruin signs marking the dirt road that leads to the hotels and the south entrance to the ruins. **Taxis** between Pisté and the ruins cost about $1.25 each way. The walk from Pisté along a roadside path to the ruins is an easy one.

TELEPHONES. Most of the hotels will handle your phone calls from their main desks; there are no phones in the rooms and no public phones in Pisté.

COBÁ

There are **tours** to Cobá from Cancún two or three times each week. The alternative is to go in your own car. Bus service is not reliable. Some small **restaurants** and **shops** are clustered at the entrance to the ruins, and there is a small entrance fee. The only **hotel** in the area is the **Villa Archeologica,** which is similar to its sister establishment in Chichén Itzá, described above.

TULUM

HOW TO GET THERE. Tulum is easily reached by rental **car** from Cancún. The **buses** traveling from Cancún to Chetumal stop regularly at the road to the ruins, and buses and **taxis** are available from Playa del Carmen, where the ferry from Cozumel lands. (See the *Caribbean Coast* chapter for information on hotels and restaurants.)

UXMAL

HOW TO GET THERE. The easiest way to fully explore Uxmal and the Mayan route is by **car**. There are numerous agencies in Mérida. Travel agents and hotels book both **bus** and **private tours** to the sites; some include dinner and a swim at a hotel by the ruins before the light-and-sound show. Public buses from Mérida reach Uxmal but do not traverse the 80-mile route past the smaller Maya sites.

ACCOMMODATIONS. There are a few good hotels in Uxmal, with swimming pools (a necessity in the sweltering heat) and restaurants, and trailers and recreational vehicles can be parked overnight at the ruins' parking lot. The number of available rooms is limited, and it is best to make reservations from Mérida. Rates for a double room range from $45 to $70 a day. There arc no restaurants in the area other than at the hotels.

Hotel Hacienda Uxmal. Just north of the ruins on Hwy. 261; 24 7142; in Mérida call Mayaland Tours, 25 2133. Lovely colonial-style building with a restaurant, swimming pool and ceiling fans. For reservations, write Box 407, Mérida, Yucatán, Mexico.

Hotel Mision Uxmal. A short walk to the ruins on Hwy. 261. Large landscaped patios, swimming pools with shaded palapas, air-conditioned rooms, restaurant and bar. Prices are usually slightly lower here than at the other hotels; 24 7308; in the U.S., call 800–431–2138.

Hotel Villa Archeologica. See Chichén Itzá above; 24 7053.

HOW TO GET AROUND. Uxmal can be reached by taking Hwy. 180 south out of Mérida, then Hwy. 261 south from Uman. To take the 80–mile loop through ruin territory continue south from Uxmal on Hwy. 261, then turn west on the paved road leading to Sayil. There are road signs directing you toward Sayil, and few other roads to confuse matters. At Oxkutzcab you can continue on the ruin road to Mani and Mayapan or hook up with Hwy. 184 toward Ticul.

USEFUL PHRASES AND VOCABULARY

Spanish is a relatively easy language to learn. Here are a few basic rules on pronunciation.

		as in:	example:
1) **Vowels** are pronounced precisely, with exceptions noted below:			
a		father	
		mas	
exception:	ai/ay	life	aire, hay
	au	out	autobós
e		then	necesito
exception:	ei	weigh	seis
	eu—no equivalent word in English, but sounds like:		**eh-ooeu**mático
i		police	repita
exception:	before a, e, o, u	yes	viaje, bien, edificio, ciudad
o		none	noche
exception:	oi	boy	oigo
u		good	mucho
exception:	before a, e, i, o	was	cuarto, puedo, cuidado, acuoso
	(silent when used with: qui, que, gul, gue)		aquí, queso, guía, embrague
2) **Consonants** are pronounced similarly to English, except:			
c before a, o, u		kick	casa, poco, película
before e, i		see	dice, décimo
g before a, o, u		go	gazpacho, langosta, gusto
before e, i		house	gerente, ginebra
gu		before a	guava agua
h (silent)		Esther	hablo
j		hill	mejor

ll	young	llame
ñ	onion	señor
q (always followed by silent "u")	pique	mantequilla
rr rolled	thr-r-ee	arroz
x as in English, except in a few proper names when between vowels or beginning a proper name	hut	México, Oaxaca,
	zest	Xochimilco Xochicalco
y before vowels	yet	ayer
when meaning "and"	me	y
z	lose	azul

3) **Accent marks** are used to indicate which syllable is stressed, or to distinguish between two words, i.e., el (the) or él (he).

General

Good morning/good day.	Buenos días.
Good afternoon.	Buenas tardes
Good evening/good night.	Buenas noches.
I am glad to see you.	Mucho gusto en verle.
I don't speak Spanish.	No hablo español.
Do you speak English?	Habla usted inglés?
A little bit.	Un poquito.
How do you say in Spanish?	Cómo se dice en español?
Do you understand me?	Me entiende usted?
I understand.	Entiendo.
I don't understand.	No entiendo.
What did you say?	Qué dijo usted?
More slowly, please.	Más despacio, por favor.
Repeat, please.	Repita, por favor.
Write it down, please.	Escríbalo, por favor.
I don't feel well. I am sick.	No me siento bien. Estoy enfermo.
I need a doctor.	Necesito un médico.
How are you?	Cómo está usted?
Fine. And you?	Perfectamente. Y usted?
Very good.	Muy bien.
I have the pleasure of introducing Mr. . . .	Tengo el gusto de presentarle al señor . . .
Pleased to meet you.	Mucho gusto en conocerle.
The pleasure is mine.	El gusto es mío.
Pardon me. Excuse me.	Perdóneme. Con permiso.
Do you have a match?	Tiene usted un fósforo?
Can I take your photo?	Puedo tomar su fotografía?
Where is the . . . ?	Dónde está . . . ?
I don't know.	No sé.
Where can I change my money?	Dónde puedo cambiar mi dinero?
Where do you come from?	De dónde es usted?
Can you tell me?	Puede usted decirme?

What do you wish?	Que desea usted?
What is the matter?	Que pasa?
Sit down, please.	Siéntese, por favor.
You are very kind.	Usted es muy amable.
It doesn't matter.	No importa.
Call me/phone me.	Llámeme por teléfono.
Is Mr. . . . in?	Está el Señor . . . ?
What is your name?	Cómo se llama usted?
Let's go.	Vámonos.
Good-bye.	Adiós.
Till we meet again.	Hasta la vista.
Until later/so long.	Hasta luego.
Many thanks.	Muchas gracias.
Don't mention it/You're welcome.	De nada

address	dirección
American	americano
aspirin	aspirina
better	mejor
boat/ship	barco
book	libro
bookstore	librería
boy	niño, muchacho
building	edificio
bullfight	corrida de toros
bullfighter	torero
business	negocio
chair	silla
church	iglesia
cigarette	cigarro
clean	limpio
cleaning	limpieza
come here	venga acá
come in	entre
depart	salir, partir
do	hacer
dry	seco
dry-clean	lavado en seco
expensive	caro
eye	ojo
eyeglasses	lentes, anteojos
few	pocos
film	rollo, película
find	encontrar
forbidden	se prohibe
from	de
garden	jardín
gentleman	caballero, el señor
girl	niña, muchacha
go	ir
good	bueno
guide	guía
handbag	bolsa de mano
hard	duro
heavy	pesado
high	alto
hospital	hospital
house	casa

husband	esposo
know	saber
lady	la señora, dama
look	mire, vea
look out	cuidado
lost	perdido
man	hombre
more	más
me	mi
my	mio, mia
name	nombre
new	nuevo
no more	nada más
no/non-	no
of	de
office	oficina
old	viejo
painting	pintura
please	por favor
policeman	policía
pretty	linda, bonita
quick	rápido, pronto
rain	lluvia
school	escuela
see	ver
single	solo, sencillo
smokers	fumadores
smoking	fumar
suitcase	maleta
sweet	dulce
there is, are	hay
thick	grueso
thin	delgado
time	tiempo
too	también
trip	viaje
United States	Estados Unidos
up	arriba
very, a lot	muy, mucho
wallet	cartera
watch	reloj
water	agua
weather	clima
welcome	bienvenido
wet	mojado
wife	esposa
with	con
with me	conmigo
without	sin
woman	mujer
yes	sí
young lady	la señorita
your	su

Calendar

Months (meses):

January	enero

February	febrero
March	marzo
April	abril
May	mayo
June	junio
July	julio
August	agosto
September	septiembre
October	octubre
November	noviembre
December	diciembre

Days (dias):

Monday	Lunes
Tuesday	Martes
Wednesday	Miércoles
Thursday	Jueves
Friday	Viernes
Saturday	Sábado
Sunday	Domingo

Year (año)

next year	el año que viene (or: el año próximo)
last year	el año pasado

Seasons

winter	el invierno
spring	la primavera
summer	el verano
fall	el otoño

Time (tiempo)

At what time?	A qué hora?
What time is it?	Qué horas son?
It's 10 A.M.	Son las diez de la mañana.
It's noon.	Son las doce.
It's 1 o'clock	Es la una.
It's 3:15.	Son las tres y cuarto.
It's 4:30.	Son las cuatro y media.
It's 5:45.	Son las seis menos cuarto.
It's 6:50.	Faltan diez para las siete.
At 8 o'clock sharp.	A las ocho en punto.
About 9 o'clock.	Cerca de las neuve.
At 10 P.M.	A las diez de la noche.
It is midnight.	Es la medianoche.
I will be a little late.	Llegaré un poco tarde.
Whenever you please	Cuando guste.
In a little while.	Dentro de poco.
minute	minuto
hour	hora
ago	hace
2 days ago	hace dos días
today	hoy
tomorrow	mañana
day after tomorrow	pasado mañana
yesterday	ayer

day before yesterday	anteayer
morning	mañana
afternoon	tarde
night	noche
for tonight	para esta noche
last night	anoche
week	semana
next week	semana próxima
last week	semana pasada
when?	cuándo?
now	ahora
late	tarde
early	temprano
next time	la próxima vez
how long	cuánto tiempo?
always	siempre
in a minute	en un momento

Hotel (hotel)

Where is the hotel?	Dónde está el hotel?
Where is a first-class hotel?	Dónde está un hotel de primera clase?
Where is a motel?	Dónde está un motel?
Where is the inn?	Dónde está la posada?
I would like a single room	Quiero un cuarto sencillo.
I would like a double room.	Quiero un cuarto para dos.
I would like a room with twin beds.	Quiero un cuarto con camas gemelas.
I would like a room with double bed.	Quiero un cuarto con cama matrimonial.
I would like a room with bath.	Quiero un cuarto con baño.
I would like a room with shower.	Quiero un cuarto con regadera.
I would like a room with a bathtub.	Quiero un cuarto con tina.
I would like a room with a view.	Quiero un cuarto con vista.
I would like a room with air conditioning.	Quiero un cuarto con air acondicionado.
I would like a quiet room.	Quiero un cuarto tranquilo.
What is the price?	Cuál es el precio?
Is there a garage?	Hay garage?
Is there a laundry or dry-cleaning service?	Hay servicio de lavandería o tintorería?
Is there a pressing service?	Hay servicio de planchar?
Is there a drugstore?	Hay una farmacia?
Is there a beauty shop?	Hay un salón de belleza?
Is there a barbershop?	Hay una peluquería?
I would like a haircut.	Quiero un corte de pelo.
I would like a shampoo and set.	Quiero un champú y peinado.
May I use your telephone?	Me permite usar el teléfono?
Where is the phone?	Dónde está el teléfono?
Where is the ladies' room?	Dónde está el baño de damas?
Where is the men's room?	Dónde está el baño de caballeros?
Open the door.	Abra la puerta.
Will you please send the baggage up?	Favor de mandar subir el equipaje.
Will you please send the baggage down?	Favor de mandar bajar el equipaje.
Put it here.	Póngalo aquí.

This isn't working.	Esto no funciona.
Close the window.	Cierre la ventana.
Keep the change.	Quédese con el cambio.
My bill, please.	Mi cuenta, por favor.
key	llave

Restaurant (restaurante)

Where is a good restaurant?	Dónde hay un buen restaurante?
I reserved a table for two.	Reservé una mesa para dos.
A menu, please.	El menú, por favor.
I am hungry.	Tengo hambre.
I am thirsty.	Tengo sed.
What do you wish?	Qué desea usted?
Bring me . . .	Tráigame . . .
I like my meat . . .	Quiero la carne . . .
medium rare	media cocida
rare	término inglesa
well done	bien cocida
I would like a little more of that.	Un poco más, por favor.
The check, please.	La cuenta, por favor.

Breakfast (desayuno)

Juices (jugos)

Tomato	de tomate
Orange	de naranja
Grapefruit	de toronja
Pineapple	de piña

Eggs (huevos)

Mexican style	a la mexicana
Mexican ranch style	huevos rancheros
soft-boiled	tibios
poached	poché
scrambled	revueltos
with sausage	con chorizo
hard-boiled	cocidos
fried	fritos
omelet	omelet
with bacon	con tocino
with ham	con jamón

Bread (pan)

rolls	bolillo
sweet rolls	pan dulce
toasted	tostado
butter	mantequilla
syrup	jarabe, miel
corn griddle cakes	tortillas
crackers, cookies	galletas
French toast	pan francesa
jam	mermelada
honey	miel de abejas

Beverages (bebidas)

coffee	café

black	negro
with cream	con crema
without milk	sin leche
Sanka	Sanka
Espresso	café express
tea	té
iced tea	té helado
chocolate	chocolate
milk	leche
bottle of pure water	botella de agua pura
mineral water	agua mineral
uncarbonated mineral water	agua mineral, sin gas

Lunch (comida) and Dinner (cena)

Appetizers (entremeses)

marinated fish	ceviche
refried beans with melted cheese topping	frijoles refritos con queso
smoked salmon	salmón ahumado
fruit cocktail	coctel de frutas
baby cactus	nopalitos
avocado dip	guacamole
herring	arenques
shrimp cocktail	coctel de camarones
olives	aceitunas

Soups (sopas)

bean	de frijol
chick pea	de garbanzos
lentil	lentejas
vegetable	verduras
consomme	caldo
pea	chícharro
garlic	ajo

Fish & Shellfish (pescados y mariscos)

salmon	salmón
trout	trucha
tuna	atún
crayfish	langostino
clam	almeja
oysters	ostiones
eels	angulas
red snapper	huachinango
bonito	bonito
lobster	langosta
crab	cangrejo, jaiba
shrimp	camarrón
snails	caracoles
halibut	lenguado
smoked codfish	bacalao

Meat & Poultry (carne y aves)

tamales with beef	tamales con carne
tacos, Enchiladas, and Tostadas with chicken or beef	con pollo; con carne
chopped meat, creole style, fried	picadillo a la criolla

green bananas and rice

meatballs	albóndigas
stuffed peppers	chiles rellenos
tortillas with meat, cheese and sauce	enchiladas
chicken and rice	arroz con pollo
chicken or turkey in Mexican chocolate sauce	mole poblano or mole con pavo (or: de guajalote)

Vegetables (legumbres)

potatoes	papas
fried	fritas
with cheese	con queso
spinach	espinaca
beans	frijoles
string beans	ejotes
peas	chícharros
asparagus	espárragos
mushrooms	champiñones, hongos
carrots	zanahorias
lettuce	lechuga
radish	rábano
celery	apio
garlic	ajo
corn	elote
sweet potatoes	camotes
tomato	jitomate
rice	arroz
squash	calabaza
beets	betabeles
cabbage	col
onion	cebolla
eggplant	berenjena
cauliflower	coliflor
sauer kraut	choucrut
artichokes	alcachofas
avocado	aguacate

Desserts (postres)

cheese	queso
Spanish cream	natillas
custard	flan
ice cream	helado
sherbert	nieve
cake	pastel
fruit salad	ensalada de frutas
stewed fruit	compota
fruit tart	pastel de frutas
candy	dulces
pudding	pudín

Fruit (frutas)

apple	manzana
banana	plátano
strawberries	fresas
raspberries	frambuesas
pineapple	piña
coconut	coco
lime	lima

lemon	limón
papaya	papaya
melon	melón
mango	mango
guava	guayaba
grapes	uvas
watermelon	sandía
fruit cocktail	coctel de frutas
plums, prunes	ciruelas

Beverages (bebidas)

cactus plant drinks:	Tequila, Mezcal, Pulque, Margarita, Tequila cocktail
beer	cerveza
Bohemia	(light, native)
Carta Blanca	(light, native)
Dos Equis XX	(dark, native)
brandy	brandy
champagne	champaña
cider	sidra
gin	ginebra
wine	vino
white	vino blanco
red	vino tinto
Spanish wine punch	Sangría
rum	ron
soda	soda, Tehuacán
sherry	jerez
liquor	licor
soft drinks	refrescos
ice	hielo

Miscellaneous

sugar	azúcar
salt	sal
pepper	pimienta
mustard	mostaza
oil	aceite
vinegar	vinagre
butter	mantequilla
knife	cuchillo
fork	tenedor
spoon	cuchara
teaspoon	cucharita
sauce/gravy	salsa
tip	la propina
waiter	el mesero
waitress	la mesera; señorita
sour	agrio
spicy	picante

Mail (correo)

post office	oficina de correos
stamps	timbres, estampillas
airmail stamp	timbres, estampillas de correo aéreo
register	registrado
letter	carta

postcard   tarjeta postal

Getting Around

By car (por carro)

How do you get to . . . ?	Cómo se va a . . . ?
Where are you going?	A dónde va usted?
How far is it to . . . ?	Qué distancia hay a . . . ?
It is near/very near.	Está cerca/Está muy cerca.
It is far/very far.	Está lejos/Está muy lejos.
Which way?	Por dónde?
This way/that way.	Por aquí/Por allí, Por allá.
Go straight ahead.	Vaya usted derecho.
Turn right/left.	Doble usted a la derecha/a la izquierda.
Keep to the right.	Tome su derecha.
When are you returning?	Cuándo volverá usted?
Is the road paved?	Está pavimentado el camino?
No parking.	Se prohibe estacionarse.
Maximum speed.	Velocidad máxima.
Go ahead.	Siga
Stop	Pare, alto

By air (por avión)

We want a reservation.	Queremos una reservación.
One way.	Viaje sencillo.
Round trip.	Viaje redondo.
When does the plane leave?	A qué hora sale el avión?
When does the plane arrive?	A qué hora llega el avión?
Is the plane on time?	Llega el avión a tiempo?
Is the plane late?	Llega tarde el avión?
No smoking.	Se prohibe fumar.
Check my luggage, please.	Revise mi equipaje, por favor.
airline	línea aérea
airport	aeropuerto
flight	vuelo

By train (por tren)

Where is the railway station?	Dónde está la estación de ferrocarriles?
train	tren
timetable	itinerario
conductor	conductor
What is the fare?	Qué es la tarifa, por favor?

INDEX

Index

Fodor's Travel Guides

U.S. Guides

Alaska
Arizona
Boston
California
Cape Cod
The Carolinas & the
  Georgia Coast
The Chesapeake
  Region
Chicago
Colorado
Disney World & the
  Orlando Area

Florida
Hawaii
The Jersey Shore
Las Vegas
Los Angeles
Maui
Miami & the Keys
New England
New Mexico
New Orleans
New York City
New York City
  (Pocket Guide)

New York State
Pacific North Coast
Philadelphia
The Rockies
San Diego
San Francisco
San Francisco
  (Pocket Guide)
The South
Texas
USA
The Upper Great
  Lakes Region

Virgin Islands
Virginia & Maryland
Waikiki
Washington, D.C.

Foreign Guides

Acapulco
Amsterdam
Australia
Austria
The Bahamas
The Bahamas
  (Pocket Guide)
Baja & the Pacific
  Coast Resorts
Barbados
Belgium &
  Luxembourg
Bermuda
Brazil
Budget Europe
Canada
Canada's Atlantic
  Provinces
Cancun, Cozumel,
  Yucatan Peninsula
Caribbean
Central America
China

Eastern Europe
Egypt
Europe
Europe's Great
  Cities
France
Germany
Great Britain
Greece
The Himalayan
  Countries
Holland
Hong Kong
India
Ireland
Israel
Italy
Italy's Great Cities
Jamaica
Japan
Kenya, Tanzania,
  Seychelles
Korea

Lisbon
London
London Companion
London
  (Pocket Guide)
Madrid & Barcelona
Mexico
Mexico City
Montreal &
  Quebec City
Morocco
Munich
New Zealand
Paris
Paris (Pocket Guide)
Portugal
Puerto Rico
  (Pocket Guide)
Rio de Janeiro
Rome
Saint Martin/
  Sint Maarten
Scandinavia

Scandinavian Cities
Scotland
Singapore
South America
South Pacific
Southeast Asia
Soviet Union
Spain
Sweden
Switzerland
Sydney
Thailand
Tokyo
Toronto
Turkey
Vienna
Yugoslavia

Special-Interest Guides

Bed & Breakfast
  Guide to the Mid-
  Atlantic States

Bed & Breakfast
  Guide to New
  England
Cruises & Ports
  of Call

A Shopper's Guide
  to London
Health & Fitness
  Vacations
Shopping in Europe

Skiing in North
  America
Sunday in New York
Touring Europe